COLLECTED WORKS FOR PERFORMANCE

COLLECTED WORKS FOR PERFORMANCE
HANNAH NICKLIN

A CONVERSATION WITH MY FATHER
SONGS FOR BREAKING BRITAIN
EQUATIONS FOR A MOVING BODY

OBERON BOOKS
LONDON

WWW.OBERONBOOKS.COM

First published in 2016 by Oberon Books Ltd
521 Caledonian Road, London N7 9RH
Tel: +44 (0) 20 7607 3637 / Fax: +44 (0) 20 7607 3629
e-mail: info@oberonbooks.com
www.oberonbooks.com

A catalogue record for this book is available from the British
Library.

PB ISBN: 9781783197361
E ISBN: 9781783197378

Cover: photo by Giulia Delprato
        design by Konstantinos Vasdekis

Printed and bound by 4edge Limited, Essex, UK.
eBook conversion by Lapiz Digital Services, India.

Visit www.oberonbooks.com to read more about all our books
and to buy them. You will also find features, author interviews
and news of any author events, and you can sign up for e-news-
letters so that you're always first to hear about our new releases.

Contents

Introduction

Storm Katie blustered its way through the South of England the evening of the 27th into the light hours of the 28th March 2016. In the little bit of South London which I currently sit, and that I call 'home' (for now) it blew. No doubt diffused slightly by the confusion of buildings and tarmac but still strong, still in that way which left me unsettled. The sound and the fury of it a kind of size that reminded me that I am small and human; safe now, but not always. No work is made in isolation. No word written without context. It is with this thought in mind that I begin this introduction by telling you about this storm, Storm Katie.[1] It kept me awake. It made me feel things about spring, and endings that come with beginnings. And beginnings that end and bring something new: broken branches and the buds that replace them. March, contrary to the old rhyme, went out like a lion. And it finds me writing these words heavy-eyed and with the sense of marking a season passed, and beginning something new.

This book is a collection of three pieces for performance that I made in collaboration with a series of other artists, musicians and people in the street from around 2012 to 2015. I feel, in 2016, my practice changing and re-shaping – not retreating from the questions at the heart of these pieces, but finding new ways of posing them through an increasing involvement in video games, and in struggling with the complex questions of art-as-activism. This feels, therefore, like an apt moment to mark what has passed, and begin some new thinking.

---

[1] Which immediately marks this writing as happening after the point at which the Met Office decided to institute a methodology of naming storms – we're only at the beginning of the first run through the alphabet though, heady days.

The subject matter of these three pieces, when presented together, could feel incongruous, but to me, they're all united by something the (formidable and brilliant) Annabel Turpin once described to me as "a deep interest in a particular audience". I might phrase it a bit differently (not being a venue programmer, for whom audiences must always be foremost in the mind) and use the word 'community'. The pieces are united by having a particular community (or communities) at their heart. Simply considered, that's the activist community in *A Conversation With My Father* (but also the police, and fathers and daughters), the punk community and the inhabitants of certain cities in *Songs for Breaking Britain*, and those who do endurance sport in *Equations for a Moving Body*. But obviously the truth is more complex and I hope that anyone outside of those communities will also find a general human-ness about the stories. In fact, that's the point.

When I talk about what I make I tend to call it 'community storytelling'. I call it storytelling rather than theatre because when I'm on the street stopping someone as they try and cross to the market on their lunch break, 'theatre' doesn't cut it. For some makers that would be the *point* of using the word 'theatre' – to explain and open up and reclaim it from the idea of it being what theatre was a hundred years ago, and still is sometimes today; heavy red curtains, proscenium arches, people pretending you're not there while they have a difficult time in a variety of accents.[2] However the *theatre* isn't the point of my theatre, people are. So I use the word 'story'. 'This is a story about' or 'have you got 5 minutes to tell me a story?'. There's something about the latter phrase that almost always makes people pause. When I'm tramping

---

[2] Of course this theatre is useful and important in different ways, but we don't need to make room in our heads for this version of theatre, it's already there.

the streets of whatever Northern city I've forgotten is Quite Cold Actually[3] in search of people with a little time to join in, 'story' catches people. It doesn't sound like a thing you sell.[4] And it's weird. It's a weird thing to ask someone.

The academic in me (or rather, my excellent PhD supervisor, Dr Dan Watt, whom I often hear in my head, challenging me to be more rigorous) demands that I pick up on the word 'community' and offer some kind of definition. It's a useful impulse, I think, to define this in particular as a way of introducing my practice. Because in the neo-liberal context of Cameron's 'big society', and in the context of the employment of 'community' to mean 'interest group' or 'nebulous collection of people we the news media have decided to designate as a community based on their non-white-straight-maleness' – the notion of 'community' has come to be instrumentalised. Sort of, I might suggest, the opposite of weaponised: numbed of everything beautiful and difficult about it. In the same way as in the other half of my practice, games (videogames primarily) and games mechanics have been instrumentalised by the 'games for good' and 'games for change' movements which often parody game systems and mechanics ('gamify') in order to produce a certain kind of behaviour, outcome, or citizen. In that same way, community has had its radical potential – the emergent and unknown – smashed out of it through instrumentalisation: by anyone who every claimed a community *did*, *thought*, or *felt* a single thing.

---

[3] 'I'm from the North' I often think (critic and blogger extraordinaire Meg Vaughan often pulls me up on this, I'm not, I'm from the middle of Lincolnshire), 'It can't be that cold in Newcastle/Stockton/Leeds etc'. It is. It is always cold. It does not help that I always seem to make new shows in Autumn/Winter.

[4] Ha. Also, "If you are in advertising, kill yourself" is honestly the most boring bit of comedy I ever heard.

What do I mean by the radical potential of community? I find the answer in the same place as I do for politics: they are a practice. A system of relationships and rules from which a doing is emergent. The radical potential of community can be found in its *doing* not its *being*.

For me, politics is not just that which politicians do, but a wider *process* – one bound up in and expressed through how we relate to one another; inherent, too, in our ideas of 'community' – how we do together. The political implications of late capitalism, for example, are overtly emergently systematic – they are continually revised and pervasive, making and remaking themselves daily – taking things meant to push against it and turning them into... pop punk, sanctioned graffiti on the hoardings of new housing developments, advertisements for butter. The capitalist system is so effective precisely because of its ability to adapt and thus to continually resist (or, more typically, subsume) practices which might attempt to oppose it.

Basically I reckon that two of the most difficult and also game-changing books I ever read were Maurice Blanchot's *The Unavowable Community* and Jean-Luc Nancy's *The Inoperable Community*.[5] That's where I found these ideas perfectly, difficultly expressed. In The Inoperable Community, we find the political defined as 'the place where community [...] is brought *into play*' (Nancy, 1991, p. xxxvii). In systems of power and influence communities are inculcated, created, and influenced. So if the political is where community is brought into play, it is also through reflection on community that politics might be *played with*. Politics is inscribed in community – and so by considering the community, our practice of politics might be considered, revisited, revised. Likewise, if politics is concerned with systems of power and

---

[5] I'm going to be cribbing a little from my PhD here, but to be honest, not even my mum has read that. So we're probably OK.

influence that essentially work with human beings as their contents, then the rules of these systems might be examined and *corrupted* by us, as well as the machine of capital. We can introduce new experimental rules, new viral transmissions of the praxis of relationships and existence, new stories. New play. The question "what-if?" asked not once, but again, and again, and again.

So I believe politics is a practice.[6] A ruleset in play – and as per games theory, the complications that arise from the playing cannot be predicted from the initial ruleset.[7] For this reason to disrupt, resist or reclaim politics and community we must do so in *practice*, by playing out their consequences rather than attempting to pin them down. 'Pinning down' is impossible, because at that point of pinning the system ceases to exist. This 'pinning down' is when the language of politics[8] attempts – and fails – to speak that which cannot be spoken; like describing a third dimension when you've only ever inhabited two. That's why those two books by Nancy and Blanchot are about the unspeakable, the impossible. They are interested in gestures towards the limit of possibility: between the limit of where I end and you begin.

This 'limit' of community is where Nancy finds 'that way of destining ourselves in common that we call a politics, that way of opening community to itself, rather than to a destiny or to a future' (Nancy, 1991, pp. 80-1). It is a 'limit' because it is the point at which community is constantly made,

---

[6] Not a system considered as a 'product' or specific end (systems of control might aspire to this, but stationary systems are always defeated by the realities of complexity, entropy; the laws of motion that govern all systems in our universe), but a self-defining and constantly re-worked inscription of political inhabitation and relation.

[7] Conway's *Game of Life* is a classic example of this.

[8] Inscribed by the actions and reactions of human beings, together.

practiced. At once born and dying, always, in order that it might live – situated in the impossible communion (meeting, talking, being together) between the subject and the other. It is a recognition of the same in the different, a notion of habitation in something which one can never inhabit. It is in this constant flux, this *in between* of your experience and mine; of my story, and your attempt to understand it, that I find something that excites me. Something exciting at the centre of the make-believe we call 'games' or 'theatre' or 'story'. That's where I find the radical heart of these practices, and it is an unproductive radical impossibility. Something complicated, inextricable.

The mainstream media are palpably eager to simplify complication, and in that context anything complicated is resisted as elitist or out of touch, or simply 'not true' because the complicated admits uncertainty. Any political presences that cannot trade in the way media prefers, such as the collective Occupy movement of the early 2010s, are therefore dismissed as 'having no aims'. Just as we see how the notion of 'truth' itself being most rigorous in constant revision is laughed at: 'what will the scientists say gives us cancer next?' While it is precisely in Occupy's *occupation* – complicated and persistent presence – that it found its power, that signified their on-going resistance, *especially* to the media. While the idea of a complicated and continually revised 'truth' doesn't have to be hard to understand if you allow it to be in flux: a process of holding and considering, and of doing that same thing again tomorrow.

I say all this stuff about the 'limit' and of 'practice' because it helps me talk about what I mean when I talk about community, and about my work. Of what I mean when I say 'if I make any kind of theatre, it is a contemporary kind of community theatre'.

Raymond Williams' definition of 'community' used by Baz Kershaw as part of his study of British Radical Theatre and its political effectiveness is of a 'medium of face-to-face interactions through which we transact ideological business with the wider social structure' (Kershaw, 1992, p. 29).[9] For Kershaw, community is what arises from the interactions between people, and in that fact is the basis of a transaction between the individual and the wider social and ideological structures in which they are implicated.[10] Obviously, though, as a Gen-Y/Millennial[11] hybrid I reject the idea that a community need be a 'face-to-face' experience. Community can also be built out of non-proximate relationships – online relationships, for example. Community is, however, like politics, a social practice: something doing, something making between us.

Victor Turner says in *Ritual, Play and Performance*:

> The social world is a world in becoming, not a world in being [...] That is why I am a little chary of the terms 'community' or 'society,' too, though I do use them, for they are often thought of as static concepts. (Turner, 1976, p. 98)

[9] There is a slight difficulty with the use of the word *transact* in Williams' definition – the exchange of one thing for another – as the community does not trade necessarily in finite artefacts or ideas, and the process of 'exchange' here is a complicated one. Although the community can be said to *arise* from the finite (or at least the experience of finitude as per 'the limit'), it is the muddy, complex impossibility of finitude that the community characterises. For me, it's about not the offering of one thing for another, but the hot space in between finite things: exchange-space, (not the items or ideas being exchanged).

[10] Ideological' here stands for all manner of social, political, religious and philosophical relationships that are created, maintained and disrupted in the space of community.

[11] All of the job insecurity, none of the innate computer skills.

That's what I'm leading us away from. When I talk about community, or politics, or theatre, I'm trying to get away from these things as static concepts.

So that's why I turn to Nancy and Blanchot. For these two community is a route to (and arises from) the encounter with our self and others-as-real-and-whole-as-us, a relationship that fundamentally brings the subject to a relationship with their own finitude (where I end, and you begin; what I know, and what I can never know, about your experience). The individual is made aware of their limits in the moment they attempt to transcend them. Nancy talks about the extreme version of this realisation of finitude when he talks about being present with someone at the moment of their death, Blanchot discusses the same impossible communion between lovers. The impossible drive to *be whole with* that is the heart of love, and the impossibility of travelling with someone at the point of death, both speak of our limits as beings, and allow us to recognise *being* in others.

I also think of the beautiful *Hedwig and the Angry Inch* song "The Origin of Love". The song is based on Plato, I think, although it is a playwright, Aristophanes, who Plato is quoting. He explains how long ago humans were double sided creatures. Great rolling things of three different forms: male-male, female-female, and male-female. And they were so beautiful and happy, not knowing love but the feeling at the completion of love – a totalness – that the Gods became jealous. Zeus decided to punish the rolling chubby happy humans, so he split us all straight down the middle. A great bolt of lightning struck us from our other half. In *Hedwig…* the title character sings about this moment. I'd like to replicate the lyrics for you here, but it would cost me and Oberon Books more money than we can afford to do so. So take a moment, and search for 'Hedwig Origin of Love', and watch the video for the song.

...

That song in some ways (and the Plato's idea in general) could be seen as an argument for their being 'The One'. But for me, it's not about that, it's about the act of love. Of Making love. Of being and doing. Of trying to thrust ourselves into a kind of communion. We can never achieve community, just as we can never achieve love. It is a process, a practice, a *doing word*. A perfect impossible thing.

When I talk about community, I talk about a practice that is not a producer of a product, but one that arises from a relationship with others, inhabited moment-by-moment. This is the radical implication of community – that when defined in terms of the encounter of the *in between* at the limits of the relationship between 'self' and 'other' it is able to shake off 'productive' ideologies. This practice of community does not create a work; it achieves nothing and is constantly rebuilt. Nancy finds in community 'that way of destining ourselves in common that we call a politics, that way of opening community to itself, rather than to a destiny or to a future' (Nancy, 1991, pp. 80-1). There we can find an inscription of 'infinite resistance' (ibid): in re-presenting and considering ourselves as part of a constant mutual inscription on and with the bodies of our selves and others. How am I like you? How am I different to you? How do I affect you? How do the things you do affect me? How can we affect the way these things work? What do we do today? How can we ask this again tomorrow? Together?

When I make work, when I make work with and for a community, I often mean a place and a collection of people, but most of all I am interested in different constellations of between: between you and me. Between the word and the meaning. Between the idea and the action. Between the performance and the audience. Between the story and the telling. That is also why there is such a focus on process when I set out to make a work – these pieces are interested in exploring ideas *in practice*. And do so by: being based on a conversation between supposedly opposing sides; going out into the street and talking to people, and collaborating with a band based on those answers; training for and completing a long-distance triathlon. And the works themselves shift in response to each audience, are never wholly scripted, always in flux.

Those are the things that I believe unite these three pieces for performance. Three works made between 2012 and 2015. Finally, I should say: these are the pieces most possible to put on a page. Missing are things like: seven installations for a swimming pool in Shipley *(Northern Big Board)*, a story game built from the stories of a housing estate in Poplar *(Teviot Tales)*, a piece for listening to on a particular park bench in Lincolnshire *(Your Home from Here)*, a card game for understanding what it is to live on minimum wage based on the stories of Stratford library users *(Another Postcode)*, a durational story-collecting game based on play and games from our past *(Games We Have Known and Loved)*, and many other bits and bobs that will never be put on paper.

These three pieces are presented on the page largely as the scripts that I work from for performance, but that in itself still presents some challenges or discrepancies from how it actually plays out on stage. For this reason each piece has an introduction, and additions and expansions that will hopefully be truer to the *practice* of the piece. They should feel, I hope, like the stories for performance with something else added, not just the words with the performance taken away.

And finally, thanks to the many people who have helped me do this, who have sent in little extras, and commentaries, and thoughts. And all of the people and organisations that helped me make the performances themselves (and develop my thoughts around them) in the first place. Let's thank them here, where they can be seen:

Thank you,

Alex Kelly, Hilary Foster, Rachael Walton, Pat Ashe, Kris Rowland, Roger Nicklin, Lawrence Nicklin, Linda Nicklin, John Helps, Tom Cassidy, Emily Chappell, Sarah Partington, Angela Hibbs, Phil Hayes, Liam Barrington-Bush, Simon Ward, Hannah Jane Walker, Chris Goode, Chris Thorpe, Lucy Ellinson, Julia Taudevin, Kieran Hurley, Nikki Pugh, Annabel Turpin, Emma Adams, Keir Cooper, Gloria Lindh, Rajni Shah, Sean Arnold, Dan Watt, Michael Parkin, Alan Lane, Michelle Walker, ARC Stockton, Contact Theatre Manchester, HUB in Leeds, Carriageworks in Leeds, Sheffield Theatres, Northumbria University, Loughborough University, Embrace Arts, Ovalhouse Theatre, HATCH Nottingham, Sheffield University, Northern Stage, Theatre in the Mill, and the Arts Council England and the Wellcome Trust.

A Conversation with my Father

Introduction

I can remember voicing the idea for this piece to my Dad for the first time in a pub called The Orange Tree in Loughborough sometime around the first year of my PhD. My brother and dad were visiting me, and we were having a conversation about the use of Tasers in policing. I thought it would be interesting, to make something that was a conversation between me, a protestor, and my dad, who had policed protest and riots as part of his 30+ years in the police service. I don't know if I necessarily thought it was going to be a piece of theatre, but I booked a room, and 3 cameras from the university, and arranged the conversation.

H K Nicklin   *24/10/2011*

to rogernicklin, rogernicklin

Hello! Just to confirm that I've booked us a room on Loughborough campus 4-6pm on the 7th of November, I know it's a bit late, but it's the only 2 hour slot they had. You'd be very welcome to come over a little earlier for a late lunch before we start?
Hope all is well in France,
Hannah xx

Roger's Hotmail   *30/10/2011*

to me

Hi

That seems ok will call you later.

Love Dad

The conversation with my dad

The conversation itself is pretty well represented in the text, so I won't elaborate on it much more here. Except to say how grateful I am for my dad's openness to the both the idea and the process of talking about these things. I am very much who I am (and proud of that) because of the kind of people my parents are: open, inquisitive, and willing to believe they can understand and achieve something if they just give it time.

Working with Alexander Kelly

After I had the recording, I decided to pitch making a performance-lecture style 20 minute piece for Hatch: Nottingham – a night of early works in progress of performance and live art. I took the recording of my dad, transcribed it, and then took the most interesting/affecting bits and stuck them in a document. I then wrote around those documents until it told the story that I felt was there. I used a Keynote presentation to show video and audio clips. The 3 video cameras had failed almost entirely (in a series of freak occurrences that astonished the Loughborough University tech department as much as me), so in the end what I had to work with was audio, from the back up mic I put on the table between us. In the parts of the text I wrote, where my father's words are there (in bold), I would play that audio excerpt via the Keynote presentation.

Following the Hatch: Nottingham work in progress showing, had a 20-30 minute piece of performance, albeit that was sort of more like a presentation than anything theatrical. It was around this time I said – sort of cheekily and not quite realising I was serious until I said it – to Alexander Kelly of Third Angel, that he should work with me to develop it into a 'full' piece. I realised I felt like he was the right person to do this, not just because of his gentle and rigorous autobiographical solo shows made with Third Angel, but also because he is a father of two young girls. It felt like a useful fit. Alex agreed to come on board as a mentor to the show and process, and Hilary of Third Angel also played a massive role in helping me write my first Arts Council England (ACE) application, and in designing a making process and supporting budget. A note should also go here for Annabel Turpin of ARC in Stockton, who emailed me around this time with a unicorn of an offer that basically went 'I've heard about your work and you seem interesting, I would like to offer you some space and a little money'. Without that, my future would have been different. As it was, it made an excellent basis for a strong ACE application, and with the support of ARC, Sheffield Theatres, Third Angel, Embrace Arts (Leicester) and Theatre in the Mill (Bradford), Alex and I set out to make the show.

Alex is a brilliant, kind and supportive mentor and devisor/ director/dramaturg. With an incredibly light touch he was able to introduce me to the experience of devising as opposed to writing (a medium I was much more comfortable in, having trained as a playwright). For those of you who don't know, devising to playwriting is like what bands do compared to a composer writing for an orchestra – when a band get a drummer and a keyboard player and a guitarist and singer together, they jam. They try out rhythms and riffs, and melodies and lyrics. That way of sculpting as you go, of play, is how devising tends to work. You'll give yourself rules, or tasks, or prompts, and try telling a story only using the third person, or silently only using images you can Google, or by building something, or by never using someone's name. Little restrictions that reveal and illuminate. Alex led me through that process and out of it. We expanded on the sections I already had, and discovered new ones. My dad visited one more time, in the week were in Leicester. And just chatted some more, answered Alex's questions, talked about some of the stories Alex had cajoled out of me. We tried several different structures for each of the sections, and inevitably struggled to cut some material, which I don't even remember now.

It was at the end of the third week of making (there were 4 weeks, officially) in Sheffield that I worked out the order. Having made 3 shows involving Alex now, he has commented that there's always a point of the process where he sees a glint in my eye, steps back, and watches me move all of the post-its or index cards until the structure reveals itself. This is a thing I'm good at, seeing the structure that leavens the story. I enjoy those moments.

The staging

A note on the staging. It's not 100% clear from the text, but in setting up the situation of the interview room, I also build it. Out of a table, two chairs, and with how I move around and inhabit the space. A big change Alex suggested for the staging was to *make* the interview room, not just talk about it. So instead of standing to one side when my dad talks, I return to 'my' chair, I sit at the table, I look at where he 'is', and I listen to him. I mimic occasional sounds, laughter and movements that you hear in the audio (all of the video, audio and photographs are controlled by a clicker in my hand/pocket). There are also certain places on stage which are 'non-interview room' positions. There's a 'lecture' position, upstage, to the left of the screen. There's a kind of invisible alley out front where I talk directly to the audience. I also sit and turn out away from 'my dad' in the chair that's mine. There's only one moment when I sit in my father's chair, and it's significantly chosen.

A CONVERSATION WITH MY FATHER

How I've chosen to present it, here.

What you're about to read is the most 'scripty' of the pieces I'm presenting. It has my words in normal text, the recording of my dad transcribed in bold in the places where I play the recordings, and minor 'stage directions' to explain when I move places. I've put the images in from the slideshow at the moments when I would click them up, and screen capped the videos so you get a sense of them.

When thinking about how I should present the performance to you in the book my first thought was to annotate it with all the places where my thoughts have changed: where I would have asked different things, where I might have said something harder, or more challenging to the audience (not, I think, to my father). But then I realised that's a different piece. There is another *A Conversation With My Father* which is with my more radical self now. A conversation that happens in the wake of Black Lives Matter, in the revelations of state-sanctioned rape and deception committed by undercover officers in the UK radical left, that happens as the police is privatised, as the anger promised in the protests that I took part in around the coalition government collapsed into exhaustion under a constant barrage of vindictive and callous governance. There is a me, now, that hears someone in certain circles say 'all cops are bastards' and understands the necessity for some people to wield that rhetoric as a weapon, in self-defence.

So I haven't written a second *Conversation*. Instead, I've handed it back to my dad. I've invited him to annotate the script. He spoke to me, I told the story of that, and then here, he's reflected on it. That seemed right. So as well as my text, you will also see footnotes, which are his reflections on reading the piece, 4 years after I made it.

My dad came to see the performance at HUB in Leeds, with my brother, just after I finished making it. They sat a chair apart, mid way back, to my left. I saw that both of them had cried when I finished the piece. I'm not sure how I felt about that. I didn't want to make them sad. I was glad, though, very glad, to be able to say the final line of the show, to my father.

Notes from my dad, before reading.

He has provided the following 3 photos – extras to supplement the ones I used. With a particular note regarding the car: a 'Volvo 360 GLT' – in the piece there is a photo with my dad, brother and me in front of a black Volvo. I describe it as the car my dad bought with the money he earned policing the miner's strikes. In fact, it turns out that black Volvo was the car *after* the Volvo he bought with that money. He was concerned that someone might read the text and spot that the Volvo pictured was a registration mark that post-dated the miner's strikes. At least, my dad is exactly the kind of person who would make that observation. I think I would still perform the show with the original photo though. Because it's true enough for theatre, and it would allow me to make a joke about the correction I've since received. The last note about the show from me is that it very much relies on a mix of ad-libbed and scripted light little jokes. It's a heavy and complicated interwoven story – as a performer, my relationship with you, the audience, is the thing that holds it together.

A CONVERSATION WITH MY FATHER

*Me as a baby,
with my dad*

My dad in uniform

*The aforementioned
Volvo*

A Conversation with my Father

Version 4 – Sheffield/February 2013

Props/Settings List

Small square table
3 chairs
Small wallet photos either 1) of Hannah and Roger 20
    years ago, or 2) of Hannah and Roger a couple of
    years ago. 1 for each member of the audience.
Pen (biro, black)
A4 paper
Sound recorder
Backpack containing:
— thermos
— water bottle
— bust sheet
— £5 note
— wallet
— backup mobile
— camera
— pink buff
— hat
— jacket
— trainers
— sandwich/roll
— snack bars
— (non-permanent) marker pen
— wet wipes
— ibuprofen
— toilet roll
Laptop & VGA adapter
Remote
Video Projector
Screen/white wall
Sound PA & 3.5mm audio jack

Hannah is onstage as the audience enter, she smiles and greets people as they come in, sat on the table to stage right. She'll encourage people to sit to the front. Chat about the weather, or generally about the city she's in. General friendly babble. Eventually the lighting will change to an 'onstage' setting. But throughout the performance the audience will be gently lit, enough that Hannah can see them when she tells the story. The headings in this text represent sections of the text for easy reference when devising and rehearsing, and aren't projected or spoken. There is a screen behind the scene which is blank at the beginning, there is a laptop visible at the back of the stage running the slides in Keynote. Hannah has a small remote in her pocket.

Hannah is dressed smartly in jeans, vest top, and a blazer, plus desert boots. If her hair is long when she performs the show, it's tied up. She's wearing glasses.

Introducing the room

As Hannah talks she sets the room up, primarily by walking around the space, but also by placing the table, two chairs, a pen and sheet of paper, and the microphone.

It's Monday the 7th of November, 2011, and the time is 4P.M. It's roughly half a year since Bin Laden was killed in Pakistan, a couple of months after the UK riots, and Occupy St. Pauls have been in London for just over 3 weeks. I'm 26 years old, and in about 2 weeks I'll have my heart broken by a boy called John. It's edging towards winter, it's cold and getting dark outside.

It's Monday the 7th of November, 2011, and the time is 4pm.

We are in a black box studio on Loughborough university campus that used to be called the rehearsal room, but got painted black so now it's a studio. About 15 minutes before this point my dad picked me, 3 cameras and a microphone up from my bedsit about a 5 minutes drive away and we drove on campus.

We weren't sure if we would be allowed on campus without a pass, so we spent the 5 minute drive trying to come up with good excuses for why we'd need to be there but in the end the security guard just waved us through. The remaining 10 minutes were spent getting lost on a campus that I know very well, but only by bicycle. Apparently they have these 'one way road' things now.

Anyway, we found our way to the rehearsal room in the end. Studio. I have brought my dad to this room to do an interview with him[12] – an interview about his experiences of policing, and also a conversation about it in relation to my protesting.

Now he's not used to being in black box studios, or rehearsal rooms for that matter, so he's doing what he normally does in the kind of situation that makes him feel awkward, he's trying to be useful.[13] Really, there's not much I need him to do, but he wants to help, so while I sort a table and chairs out I let him play with the lights. I only really need a light on both of our faces, which should take about 30 seconds, but I let him get it *just right*.[14]

I don't like the long tables in the room, so I push them to one side and go and get a small square table from the postgrad room down the hall.

SETS TABLE

I set it in the middle of the room, where there is now some splendid lighting, and pull up two chairs either side.

SETS CHAIR

---

[12] Scary!

[13] I have always been doing something, something is comfortable and you are my daughter, it's what (in my limited experience) I believe Dads should do.

[14] Pokes tongue out!

SETS CHAIR

My dad sits down in this chair angling himself slightly this way, while I just check over the cameras. There is a camera here, pointing at my face, here, at my dad's, and here, which captures both of us. Mostly, in fact this is the only camera that works in the end. For reasons that I won't bore you with. So the only full record of our conversation I have is from the little zoom mic that I put here. There is also a page of notes on my side of the table and a clicky pen that occasionally makes a horrible sound on the recording.

My dad sits across from me looking like the old man[15] he never is in my head. In my head he has thick black hair, strong blue eyes and a black moustache. His hair is thin and almost white in places, now, and a few years ago in a mini mid-life crisis he shaved his moustache off. Now he has this weird visible flappy top lip thing that occasionally still freaks me out. His eyes are still a blue colour, but a watery one.

My dad is wearing brown leather shoes, dark denim jeans, a light coloured shirt with the top button undone, and a thick heavy jumper over the top. He sits back, but sometimes when he's talking he leans forward and draws on the table with his finger.

I sit in this chair. I am roughly one and a half stone heavier than I am now. I'm wearing black ankle boots, thick tights, a short denim skirt, top and cardigan. My hair comes down to here, and is a darker red than it is right now and I have a fringe. I wear glasses, but because I don't want them to be in the way of me talking to my dad I take them off and put them down, here.

It's Monday the 7th of November, 2011, and the time is 4P.M. Just after.

Turn to audience

[15] **Nor me still have a younger self image but hey ho.**

I call my dad, 'daddy'

I call my dad, 'daddy'. That's just his name. I never felt the need to change it as I grew up, I've never been one of those people who shortens names, and it felt strange to call him something different just because I was getting older. Like tea and coffee. You all know they don't actually taste nice, don't you? I never felt the need to acquire their taste. I never felt the need to call my dad by anything other than his name. Daddy.

Falling asleep with colic/my brother's broken leg

Stands up,

I'm told that when I was a baby I had really bad colic. Proper up all night screaming, nightmareish first child stuff. I'm told that the only way I used to fall sleep, was lying flat on my father's chest.[16]

Hannah moves upstage right

One of the earliest memories of my dad, maybe the earliest, is of him carrying my brother home just after he broke his leg sledging down the Big Hill. My brother had considered sticking his leg out to catch on a passing lamppost[17] a reasonable way of coming to a halt. I remember my brother, high up in his arms, I remember that he was shaking.

---

[16] We tried everything laying you on sheepskin, gripe water but the only way you would sleep was laying on my tummy. I did it because mum needed her sleep having looked after you all day and still feeding you during the night. It was okay just laying there on my back waking every so often to remember not to turn over. To this day I don't sleep on my back, however you were a lovely hot water bottle and quiet!

[17] It was a telegraph pole and I felt really bad about it especially as I didn't think about it being broken until he didn't stop crying. Neither of you were criers (after your colic).

This is a picture of my brother just after he had the cast put on. I kind of look like I'm hurting him, but I promise that I'm just being loving.

Goodies and baddies, the Oath, the turnip incident

When my dad signed up to the police, he took an oath. This is his voice.

Hannah sits at the table, as if she is listening to her father.

There was an oath, and that was to solemnly serve our sovereign lady the Queen in the office of Constable, to basically enforce the laws of the country, without fear, favour or affection, and I always had a streak of

fairness within me[18], and again you have to look at the sort of exposure to young people of television in those days was very limited. Television wasn't on 24 hours a day, and that was limited programs, but a lot of those programs had a moral tale. *The Lone Ranger*, and the goodies always won. And I think that is what is my upbringing, in terms of expecting fairness, and to be dealt with equally. I mean as a youngster I had limited dealings with the police but I did get taken home by a[19] – the local policeman on one occasion, for doing something I shouldn't have been doing

Turns to audience

When my dad was little, he was escorted home by the local policeman,[20] for knocking that policeman off his bike with a turnip dug up from the local hospital farm.

Turns back

R: and the other thing was, now I wasn't alone obviously, but we were chopping off the heads of the turnips with a sheath knife, which one of the lads had brought along, of course I was holding one of the turnips, and the sheath knife went into my finger.

H: oh!

[18] Possibly because I had felt unfairly treated e.g. on reflection sitting the 11 Plus without any warning or preparation and being consigned to a prophecy fulfilling education, as many were.

[19] Policeman.

[20] After being taken to the hospital administrator for a dressing down, I don't think we actually knocked him off his bike, just hit him. It was a mental hospital and part of the "therapy" was for patients to work on the attached farm.

R: so as well as having to get me taken home by a police officer, mum then had to take me up to the hospital, so she wasn't very pleased

Turns to audience

He still has a scar… it's on this finger.

Hannah stands

All the images, videos and audio you hear or see today belong to or were taken by me, or my friends or family.

11 DEMOS

Miliband July 09

The first protest I ever went on was in July 2009. It was a really hot day and the protest was in the south of the country. I can't for the life of me remember where. Somewhere near the sea.[21]

[21] Here's me trying to "do something" again: if it is the linking up around the power station as per the photos then that is Kingsnorth in Kent on the River Medway estuary.

I'd made the decision to go because, while I'd always been politically interested, a few things had recently made me feel like I really needed to take action. It was a couple of plays about climate change, as well as a New Scientist issue on rising sea levels.

I come from Lincolnshire. It's a beautiful place. There's no where else like it. The horizons just sit back, and sometimes I just need to go there to ctrl alt del my mind. Pretty much most up to date climate science puts it underwater[22] within the next 50 years. Within my lifetime there's a good chance I will not be able to return to the landscape that to me, is home.

I couldn't ignore it anymore. I had to do something. At the time I wrote in a blog post "I think I want to be one of the people who gives policy a little push, along with a billion other little pushes, to make leap in the right direction, […] I'm ready to be radical. I think the time demands it". I attended my first protest 2 months later.

It was a good first protest to go on. Loads of families, stalls and musicians, friendly police who smiled at you as you went past.

It was called the 'Milli-Band' because it was when Ed Miliband was climate change secretary and the idea was 1000 (milli) or more people would hold hands (band) around a power station to protest the building of more dirty coal stations in the UK.

[22] **Where I am will be an island, part of the Isle of Axholme.**

On the train back a load of people started having a go at this really young lad, so I stepped in and stopped them, as the boy jumped off at his stop he gave me his straw hat. I still have that hat.

I have been on two protests against education cuts, in November 2010 I attended **Demo 2010** – a protest against the education cuts proposed by the coalition government. It was a big protest.

Hannah changes to a blank slide.

I walked past Millbank – Tory headquarters – just as people were starting to throw stuff. There were a lot of first time protestors, almost all under 25, lots of 16, 17 year olds protesting the removal of educational maintenance allowance. There was a real buzz I'd not felt before. People on edge, excited, not sure if they were breaking the rules, a bit scared, very angry.

I was in London for a meeting in **December 2010**, the day that the **education cuts bill** was being voted on. I heard over twitter that people were going to protest. I went. I went not because I thought I would make a difference, but because I needed to have been there, to at least have said 'stop'.

That was the first time I was kettled.

This is Millbank //video with following audio overlaid:

Hannah watches live video from her phone taken on the education cuts protest overlaid with her father's words. It is around the Millbank building, where at the moment the video was taken, people were starting to smash windows.

H: how would you describe your politics?

R: hm, I would say that I'm pretty much leaning leftwards[23],

H: and what, what's informed that in your life?

R: I think my upbringing, again, the sense of fairness, the experiences I had as a child with a family[24]. And the opportunities I also had which were afforded me which aren't present for young people today. I don't think there is the opportunity to, to develop and to move beyond your beginnings, as in opportunity, despite the two-tier education system now, I was able to move beyond that, and I had the social support systems, you

---

[23] That is that the state exists to help and support people to achieve what they can and not to exploit or manipulate them to their own selfish ends.

[24] It twas an ard life down sawf.

know social services, the support of good teachers at school, the open University, which came along. Those opportunities I benefited from,

Sense of fairness, parity

I think I realised, in talking to my dad, that actually one thing I got from him, which I always thought I got from my mother, a sense of fairness, of parity. Of seeing things from both sides. When I am at a protest and I see a line of police officers I don't see the enemy, I see a load of people with a difficult job to do and the partners and children sat at home waiting for them to come back. I don't mean to say that I'm special or good for thinking that, I mean I've been that little girl, waiting for her dad. And sure some police officers like hitting people with sticks, but you get dickheads at protests too, and in all the professions, it's just policing is the only one where you're actually given a stick.[25]

This is the blood

This is the blood of someone beaten until they were unconscious.

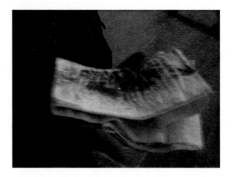

[25] **That is all part of the problem from all sides still happening all over and especially with refugees, that of de-humanisation (Allports Scale) which takes away the personal and makes someone an it or them. It is far easier the to attack and denigrate them. The same happened to the Jewish religion in WWll and continues today in conflicts through out the world.**

My father is… I am….

Hannah goes over to the back of her father's chair and holds the back.

My Father is 58, he was born in Maidstone in 1955 to a single parent and has two sisters and one brother. In the recording he doesn't mention that these, I think, were by another father. My dad never knew who his dad was. He doesn't mention that either.[26] He was brought up on a council estate,[27] attended secondary modern, and after his hopes of joining the fire service were dashed by the closing of the fire cadets, with nothing else to do at the age of 16, he joined the other thing with 'cadet' in its name: the police. At 19 he was able to join fully. He retired from the police after 31 years service in 2005.

Hannah walks to the back of her chair, and holds it. We're talking about in the interview here, not in 'real life'.

I am 28 and a quarter. I was born in Maidstone in 1984 to Linda and Roger Nicklin. I was named 'Hannah'. My mum worked with social services and my dad had been in the police 'regulars' for 10 years at that point. They met at Open University, and both had been married before. My dad's first words to my mum were 'oh, I thought you were a man'.[28] She had very short hair. I moved away from Maidstone at the age of one and a half and grew up in a farmhouse in Lincolnshire as it was being converted.

---

[26] Not sure this is deliberate. I occasionally think about what I might achieve by knowing however I don't know what I missed except one thing I am more comfortable in female company and have difficulty with macho men. I am competitive but do not like competing!

[27] They hadn't all been turned into sink estates by then.

[28] Well her hair was cropped!

I attended a local comprehensive and aside from various years out working in admin, data entry, kitchens and bars, I have studied to PhD level. Over the past 3 years I have been on 11 protests.

UAF Vs. EDL

The fifth protest I went on was a day after the fourth.

I'd already come to London for Million Women rise, and so when the next day I heard over twitter about a counter protest organised by UAF (Unite Against Fascism) against a march planned by the EDL (English Defence League) – I decided to go along. The EDL were marching in support of a Dutch politician visiting with an anti-Muslim film. At that protest, though, I realised that I don't actually think the tactics of UAF are all that useful.

The EDL had only announced their march a few days before, this, under the laws that govern protest around Westminster, meant there was no way of getting permission in time for a counter-protest. This meant that the police had carte blanche to basically arrest everyone there with UAF. They didn't. And even when they were the thin line separating the EDL on one side and the UAF on the other, as long as neither side was being violent, they let both pass.

UAF had other things in mind, though, they tried to stage a sit-in in front of the planned EDL march. They announced this quietly by word of mouth and suddenly everyone was sitting down, arms linked, and the police were faced with either letting the EDL meet them... us, or clearing the path

I was sat next to a woman who must have been in her 70s, she told me she remembered escaping Germany as a child during the war. There was also a boy near me, a young boy, college age, about 17, who was shaking. He was local, from South East London, he told me it was his first protest, that he hated the idea of the EDL walking through his city. He couldn't roll his cigarette he was shaking so badly.

UAF didn't tell these people that what they were doing was against the law. I have no problem breaking the law to stand up for things I think are right, I do have a problem with letting people do it without knowing it might get them arrested. A lot of people were. Eventually it was cleared. People chanted 'shame on you, shame on you' at the police as they dragged away each protestor. Then people moved to just outside parliament and the EDL arrived.

The video is taken from the UAF side. A hugely loud chant is heard, a woman screaming 'NAZI SCUM, OFF OUR STREETS' repeatedly, heard above the roar and occasional shout of an EDL protestor. Mounted police walk by. There are a lot of England flags, raised fists, swearing, pointed laughter, a dazed man is nearly trampled by a police horse, and then the audio fades, though the parade of EDL supporters continues.

I looked at them. Almost exclusively male, young to middle aged men. A lot of skin heads, hoodies and football shirts. I can't justify my assessment, but, instinctively, I'd say largely working class. They sneered and spat. So did the UAF. A greater mix of people, women, people of different colour, but all more eloquent, at another unsupported guess, mostly middle class, university educated. They sneered and they spat.[29]

They called the EDL 'Nazi scum' and it hurt me to hear a person call another person that – not just 'wrong' or 'racist' or 'different' – scum, below me, beneath contempt. I searched for something to shout. I tried the humiliatingly clunky 'try reading a book'. A thoughtful, quiet person next to me said 'you think they were ever given the chance?'[30] I walked away from that protest.

This is not a story about Them and Us. This is a story about a family.

For the first Time Hannah sits in her dad's chair

---

[29] **Polemics? It's the extremes, isn't it? If you get the extremes of either they can often look the same. It can make you vicious and violent. You can be morally justified, or morally unjustified, but I don't feel like the viciousness or the violence is justified.**

[30] **I wonder if that's more the point?**

CO STORY

They'd just got back from Holiday

It was Easter, and they'd been to Wales, in a caravan, where it rained a lot.

She'd listened to the sound of the rain drumming on the awning.

But now they're home, driving up the drive of their house in a village in Lincolnshire, where it had also rained a lot.

They unpack the caravan, pick the animals up from the kennels, eat their tea, and go to bed, ready to wake up back in the everyday.

She wakes up

She feels… heavy.

She turns on the light, which is just next to her bed, and swings her legs over the edge.

The girl is 5 years old, her brother, in the next room is 3, she doesn't know how old her parents are.

She feels sick.

The air feels, weird.

She gets up to go to the bathroom.

Normally she would run down the corridor that takes her there because of the crocodile that will eat you if you move too slowly but she doesn't. She can't. The air swims in front of her, she touches the wall, cream and cold.

A little way from the bathroom door, she collapses.

He wakes up.

His wife stirs next to him, mumbles something, but doesn't wake.

He realises he was woken by a thud.

He gets up.

He runs a hand over his forehead, turns on his bedside lamp, opens the bedroom door.

He finds his daughter, unconscious.

He picks her up and she stirs, says she felt sick. He carries her to the bathroom, and then goes downstairs to get her a glass of water.

He walks into the kitchen

The air feels, heavy.

He heads over to the sink, but something makes him realise that the kitten that they have that still sleeps inside at night isn't at his feet. He turns, and walks over to the cat bed, the green cat bed with the blue paisley cushion, between the heavy wooden table and the washing machine. He kneels down and puts his hand to cat.

The kitten is cold, dead.

He thinks for a moment.[31]

He goes upstairs.

He calls the doctor. 'Open the windows' she says.

He wakes his wife, and his son aged three, and takes them with his daughter and they sleep in the caravan.

"It's like an extra little bit of holiday".

The next morning the doctor calls. She tells the father 'that was terrible advice, if you'd just done that you'd all be dead'.

While the mother quietly tells the boy and the girl about carbon monoxide. About how the kitten had died but saved

---

[31] **Still remember that all so vividly, if you hadn't collapsed on the way to the bathroom and I hadn't heard you we wouldn't be here now. The silent killer. We had a solid fuel range for cooking and heating and while we were away the cold and rain had cussed soot to falling back off the chimney to the base of the flue pipe leading to carbon monoxide backing up into the house. If for not finding the kitten I would have likely gone back to bed.**

all their lives. The kitten was called Tank – named by the boy who was going through a military phase, the previous cat had been called Arun, which is a kind[32] of lifeboat – and the mother had rescued it from a dual carriage way. "It got a little bit more life, and then it gave us some" she says.

A little later they get a new cat. The boy calls it "Lucky".

Get up out of dad's chair

'Both sides of the story'

Hannah unpacks her protest gear onto the table and 'her' chair during following audio. Each item is meticulously laid out. The backpack contains:

— *thermos*
— *water bottle*
— *bust sheet*
— *£5 note*
— *wallet*
— *backup mobile*
— *camera*
— *pink buff*
— *hat*
— *jacket and fleece, on the back of the chair*
— *trainers laid in front of the chair*
— *sandwich/roll*
— *snack bars*
— *(non-permanent) marker pen*
— *wet wipes*
— *ibuprofen*
— *toilet roll*

She then lies the backpack at the side of 'her' chair, then goes to stand behind her father's chair, looking at the 'interview' as it finishes.

[32] **Type Arun Class, I know these things!**

I – I've always tried to see both sides of the story, and at any protests there is a line where you have to say right, "that's what people are allowed to do, and they're allowed to do XY and Z," be it withdraw their labour, be it peacefully picket, and try and dissuade other people from going to work, in support of their cause, and there's always an argument whether that cause is justified or not. But for a police officer if you going to deal with people impartially, then you have to say that's not an issue. And that's one of the things that the police officers, is that they're not allowed to take active part in politics. Doesn't stop them having views, obviously, it doesn't you know, stop it from obviously colouring the way they've dealt with things. But I wish that the line that, allow people to do what they could do within the law, but if the law was broken you then have to deal with that. That doesn't always mean arresting, or prison, sometimes that is words of advice, sometimes it is saying to simply "right, there's the line, you've crossed it, step back" or "this is the line, don't cross it". and it's always trying to strike that balance, because at the end of the day, the police officers have still got to police that community.[33] And that is always difficult, I don't know to this day but there are places in this country there is hatred for the police because of what happened during the miners dispute. I think that's sad, because at all times, police officers have to deal with all sorts of events and incidents that affect the community, some of which you know, are lifesaving, some of which are life changing, certainly in terms of having to deal with grief and loss, particularly in terms of road traffic collisions and stuff like that. So it's difficult, there's no simple answer, [...] I think that's the danger, and that's where a lot of police training

[33] For me it meant protecting in the widest sense so people can go about there day to day business unhindered and in safety.

school in, safely[34] in my experience, to, make people aware of the dangers of dehumanising individuals, so it becomes a 'them' and 'us', or a certain group of individuals then, because once you start saying, 'well they're not an individual, they're a group of people, and that group of people is bad, and you can treat them differently because they're bad', then you're on the road to, not discrimination, but it's on the road eventually, if you go from, obviously, name-calling and dehumanising people, you can then start behaving violently towards people. And it doesn't matter whether it's the police force, whether it's the community, or whatever, you know, if these group of people are seen to be worthless, if there's eem to be have a lesser value, then they end up eventually... like the Jewish community in the second world war.

Questions I didn't ask section

I didn't ask my dad... about his dad[35]

I didn't ask my dad... if he had hit someone, because I didn't want to be able to imagine him in that situation.

I didn't ask my dad... if he had ever lost control.[36]

I didn't ask my dad... what it felt like to strike someone

I didn't ask my dad... to strike someone on behalf of someone else. The queen. The country

I didn't ask my dad... why he left the force. But I think it's because he had a mental breakdown.[37]

---

[34] Police training is so important to ensure that officers are aware of the dangers...

[35] Not much to add I understand his name might have been Wright and he might have been in the Army Station near Maidstone

[36] Once for a few seconds and remember and regret it.

[37] Partly but more that I had reached retirement age and I had had enough of plaiting fog.

Protest gear section

Hannah sits in her chair and takes the pen, and bust sheet. She writes down the number of the legal support hotline on her forearm. Then looks up and explains what it is. Whilst dressing and packing her back, she conversationally explains what each item is/is for.

- *Thermos – hot drink if kettled on a cold night. A chance to make a callback RE the no tea or coffee thing – it's soya hot chocolate*
- *water bottle – but don't drink too much, you don't want to have to wee in a kettle*
- *bust sheet – advice for if you're arrested*
- *£5 note – would be more now, tucked into the sock in case your bag is lost/stolen/taken*
- *wallet*
- *backup mobile – for when your smart phone battery dies/is taken/is smashed*
- *camera – same as above*
- *pink buff – sometimes for warmth, sometimes to cover my face*
- *hat – same as above*
- *jacket – a two-part jacket system that is good for a little bit of light relief in this section as I can never do it up properly in front of an audience. Zips are hard when you're also trying to remember and perform things.*
- *Trainers – grippy comfy shoes*
- *sandwich/roll – probably marmite and cheese*
- *snack bars – which I'll inevitably eat before even beginning the march because they're exciting*
- *wet wipes – useful in general*
- *ibuprofen – this and above referred to as a 'mini med kit'*
- *toilet roll – for weeing in front of people, for blowing your nose, for staunching bleeding.*

Hannah now looks like a protestor. Whatever that is.

POLICE UNIFORM SECTION

This is the uniform my dad wore until 2005 when he left the force.

> *Throughout the next section, Hannah reveals each label and talks a little bit about each part of the uniform as her father has explained it to her.*

Normal uniform slide

Things to note: my dad makes reference to a series of things here which shows his very clear understanding that some coppers go out looking for violence. Some wear gloved 'even in the summer, so the bruises wouldn't show' and 'strap hangers', being what you called coppers who left the strap of their baton hanging over their baton pocket top, always ready for the

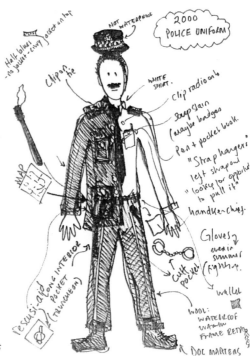

fight. He also said 'not on my watch'. In the items of the resusci-aid, and the map, there are two things increasingly forgotten in an era of smart phones and improved response times of ambulances. Clip on ties, so if someone tries to strangle you, it just comes straight off. And a pen and pocket book in your top pocket – where you write down everything you might need to refer to at a later date. The full get-up is your 'full blues', but if you take your tie, jacket and coat off, that's your 'half blues'.

Public order policing uniform slide

Great joke to begin with, here, because it is essentially a giant woollen onesie. That joke stops the monotony and the seriousness of the previous bit, and breaks it up nicely. One note here is my dad talking about the different approaches different constabularies take to policing protest – even down to whether they wear the armour on the top, or

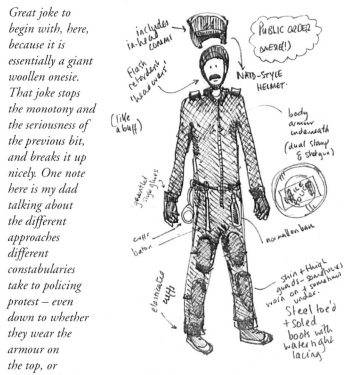

underneath the onesie – whether they want to look aggressive or not. It in some way depends where you're trained (the Met have a much more combative approach compared to people trained by Manchester. My dad said a couple of times 'the police is not the Met' – but with recent changes in training and policy, they increasingly are.

This is what my father would have been wearing if he was policing a public order incident. However when he policed his first riot it came out of nowhere, and all he had on were his full blues.

I was 3 years old when my dad policed his first riot. He was 33. 5 years older than me, now.

At time of writing, this is only 2 years older than me now, these details I always re-check and change to make them correct at the time of performance, which always makes them slightly hair raising moments. Doing up a zip, and working out how much older you are than your dad was you are now are things much harder when done in front of an audience.

This is me/this is my dad, section – 15 minutes

Each of these lines comes with a new image. I've not added in all of them, when all I did was e.g. add on an extra arrow.

This is me: //
This is my dad //
This is my dad at my age now //

This is me at my age now //
This is my dad at the age I was born (he was 30) //

This is my dad the same year that he policed his first riot //
This is me trying to escape my first kettle. //

This is the Volvo my dad bought with the overtime he earned policing the miners strikes //

This is me in a spectacular Superted jumper.[38] Learning about goodies and baddies. (And Welsh teddy bears and spotty aliens) //

This is the police officer who threatened to arrest me for wearing a pink scarf over my face. //

This scarf.

Hannah pulls up the scarf she's wearing onto her face. It covers her mouth.

[38] **Nanna Joss was a great knitter and Joss was a gentle man.**

Sergeant Hanna

The last protest I went on was **the March for the Alternative** in March 2011, a march for the alternative to the cuts; investment, short term borrowing for long term growth, green investment, that kind of thing.

About half way through we break away from the protest route. Not because we want to cause trouble or anything, but because we've been marching for *ages* and some friends of ours are performing a bit of anti-cuts street theatre further up the route and we don't want to miss it. There are about 9 of us, me and a load of people from Leeds Against the Cuts, including my friend Emma – who I have a photograph from that day of her with ice cream on her nose – and Jane, who had 'no cuts' inscribed in her homemade pasty. There was also a priest, but not one of the weird ones, one of the radical kind who wear jeans and loose shirts, with earrings and who have protested all over the world, stood in front of tanks and things.

There are about 9 of us on the walk up to Trafalgar square and the priest – who knows London well (of course he does) – says that if we cut through Horseguard's Parade we can get to where our friends are performing. So we follow him, through a mix everyday Saturday shoppers. Then we hit a wall of people, we've found the march again, but people aren't moving and something feels different about the energy of the crowd. Suddenly two people in black either side of the street scale parallel lamp posts – with proper climbing gear and everything – and string a banner up between them

It reads in red paint 'stop the cuts', we move slowly forward and see 3 people – 2 young men and a woman with dark purple hair climb out of the windows of a posh looking building to the right. They excitedly egg the crowd on, who are cheering them, then a young woman with red tights and long wavy brown hair comes out and scrawls 'tax the rich' on the side of the building in chalk.

We're at the edge but I dip into the throng to try and work out what's going on. It turns out we're outside Fortnum and Mason. Another thing I realise moving through the crowd is that police officers are inserting themselves into it, around it – you wouldn't notice if you weren't moving around like I am – there's a kettle happening.

So I duck back out, move to the edge. I want to hang around and find out what's happening but half of the people we're with aren't regular protest goers, and are a bit nervous so we move on.

I spot Forward Intelligence officers with cameras sitting back and filming everyone who passes, so I pull my scarf up over my face. And in a couple of minutes the kettle directly in the path of the agreed protest route has caused such a bottleneck, we're walking through near empty streets. The odd line of coppers offering a guard to Topshops and Vodafone stores

But apart from that, empty. Empty of traffic, empty of shoppers, filled with the subversive silence of a school corridor during class.

A call raises from far behind us. "Whose streets?" And we rally with the answer "Our streets!" "Whose streets?" "Our streets!" And then another voice "Remove your scarf" I turn,

and 2 police officers face me, one beckons. I move towards him but I don't pull down my scarf. "I'm sorry?" "Remove your scarf or I will arrest you" he says. And I do what I always do when I'm scared, I get ultra logical, I ask under what law he can threaten me with arrest for wearing a scarf over my face. He responds that under section 60AA of the criminal justice and public order act of 1994 an officer of the rank of Inspector or above can authorise the arrest of people wearing of head or facial coverings in a certain area. I take my scarf down, and I ask for his badge number, and if I can have a photograph of his badge. He allows me to – holding it up for my camera – and we joke slightly about my first name being Hannah, and his surname, Hanna.

We walk away.

My friend Emma turns to me and says "I can't believe how calm you were!"

And I want to find a way to tell her that I wasn't calm, I was scared and angry and frightened and I felt like a little girl trying to reason with an angry teacher. But I don't. I make a half-hearted joke, and then pull the scarf back up, rebelliously. Whilst hoping like hell Sergeant Hanna doesn't spot me.

Return to black.

<u>Kettling</u>

Does everyone here know what 'kettling' is?

You've probably heard the word. And it's become one of those words, that you hear, and you sort of understand in essence what is happening. If you stop and think about it. Maybe. It's a reasonably volatile sounding word, but also something quite domestic, controlled heat, controlled chaos, yes?

But then it becomes one of those words. One of those words you hear, on the news and in the papers and on facebook or twitter; like 'striver' and 'skiver' or 'Eurozone crisis/ fiscal cliff' it just becomes part of the scenery, of the news architecture. It does something, but somewhere far away.

These terms are always changed for a term relevant to the politics of the day.

Video of the Westminster student protest. It begins at dusk. A video tracking Hannah's footsteps and then as she looks around people begin to run, it's slowed down but obvious that she's running too. She's stopped. Then it cuts to later on. It's dark , the sun has set, and the video shows a line of riot police approach and then force the line of protestors back. They have large shields and wave batons.

Just in case you've not heard of it at all before, kettling a way of enclosing a group of protesters and detaining them for a number of hours.[39] Usually without food, water, shelter, or toilets. The police need no provocation to do this.

You can tell a kettle is being planned when yellow-jacketed police start hanging about in lines along streets in an area.

At this point you can probably go through. I often go up and chat to them, or ask them where the nearest bin is. Usually just to force them to see me as a person. Eventually their lines will tighten and you will be told where another way out is, there is now only one way out. This is normally where I hang about when I notice the yellow jackets tightening, so I don't see what happens to them, I suppose black-jacketed riot police might line up behind them, but now most of focus is on the way out. Mostly yellow jackets again, but you'll spot black jackets in regiments if you're paying attention. When everyone around you starts running, that's when you know it's closing down.

[39] **Never thought this was a good idea and questionably lawful.**

And you run with them, just as at least 2 lines of riot police run to form a barrier across the only way out. Last time I was kettled I made it past the first line, but not the second. You hang about feeling stupid for a bit. Until they start closing it down. The black-jacketed line moves forward and they shout 'Get back! Get back! Get back!' with their shields in front of them. If you do not move, they will hit you. I have also seen this done with horses, they ride them into the crowd. A horse stood on a girl and I saw her collarbone snap.

Once they have you in that space they will keep you there for hours. Sometimes in incredibly confined spaces, like a bridge. Where people faint but remain standing up because there's nowhere for them to collapse. There's rarely any water, or food, or toilets. It's often dark by that point, and very cold. People are angry and stifled, and scared and desperate. Some people fight the lines of police. Some people light fires with whatever they can find. It all makes very good photos for the press.

Eventually they let people go bit by bit. After they've snatched the ones they want to arrest. They often demand details to leave a kettle that you are not by law required to give.

I lied to get out of my last kettle. It was frightening.

Policing a riot

Hannah undresses, unpacks, redresses into 'normal' Hannah in the far corner, then returns to sit down when finishes.

[…] frightening. Again, a lot of things happening in your head, wondering what you should be doing, there wasn't an overall person at the scene at the time in control, so we were having to talk among ourselves, while watching what was going on to see what we're going to try and do. So part of it was gut reaction, it was frightening but in the sense that you were careful about what was coming your way, but not frightening in the sense that you didn't know that you were supposed to be there, putting a stop to it. […] we're given powers over and above ordinary citizens and those powers are ones which, along with the powers comes responsibility, you have to justify your actions to show what you're doing is legitimate, you know proportionate and necessary and you know, we were able, to use force to stop the violence. And as much force as is reasonable, and who justifies what is reasonable or not if[40] the Officer themselves before whatever tribunal; be it a Court, be it an internal investigation, that decides what Force should have been used.

[…] I think the difficulty comes in the different perceptions of the public and the police. Because I think with a clear understanding about what force is legitimate and certainly, on that night people, you know I instructed people to draw their truncheons, and use them on the, – the people that were attacking us. As a means of deterrent, and a means of controlling the situation. Now, I know I struck people with my baton that night and I know officers who got injured with bricks, and bottles, on that night. So, the difference is:

[40] 'is', I think?

one is legitimate force, and one is illegitimate force, because from my perspective we were reacting to a situation that has occurred, and we need to restore, restore order, and stop the criminal behaviour. Now, if you've got officers that are behaving criminally, you've got officers that are instigating the situation, then that's a different matter and you can understand that the reactions of the people that are subject to that, I can understand that. But that then comes down to the whole line of supervision; I mean I had 5 officers who I was responsible for that night and I made sure that they were obviously together, and that they weren't taking risks that put themselves in further danger, and also that they were behaving in accordance with the, the code of behaviour that should be there when dealing with that. And that was my responsibility to make sure, and that I think it's one of the things that over the years has deteriorated; the requirement for supervisory officers to take that role and not become one of the crowd, one of the group, but to stand back and say, "there's the line, this is what you can do, this is what you can't do, go beyond that line and you're in trouble."

Bravery

I think the think that most struck me about how he describes policing that riot in the interview, is that idea of legitimacy. It's frightening, but there's a sense of belonging there, of sanctioned purpose. When you protest, it's the opposite. You are a symbol of opposition. You don't get positive protests because they're called celebrations. So you are opposing something, and you are a power; a symbol is powerful, manipulable, sure, but potent in the moment of being made. When trouble happens I feel like I'm vibrating. Like all my atoms are vibrating a little faster. My heart beats in a way that I can feel it and my mouth is dry and I am filled with fear and sadness. Sadness when people shout 'scum' or 'pigs'. Sadness when I look into people's eyes and see hatred. Aimed at the wrong people. Aimed at the wrong people.

I have been to 11 protests in the past 3 years. Half of them did not end in disturbances. Some of them were policed really well.

At **Million Women Rise in March 2010** – an all-female march against violence against women – the Met worked with organisers to try and make sure there were as many female police officers on the cordon as possible.

And at **The Wave in December 2009** – a huge huge climate protest around the time of the Copenhagen Climate Summit -it was very quiet, and heard a police officer tell a few people in front of me to 'make a bit of noise'.

At the half that did end in disturbances, I was scared. I was constantly looking for escape routes, I didn't want to get arrested. I felt like a bad protester.

R: but is that not bravery, if you're frightened and nonetheless carry on to do what you believe in.

H: I- I- well maybe it is. I've always felt like a bad protester because of how scared I feel, like I'm, I'm not doing it right,

I lied to get out of my last kettle

It was a student protest November before last. Very cold. I was dressed smartly because I had been to a meeting earlier that morning. I was at the second line of police and they were pushing forwards. I tried to escape them by ducking in a doorway and letting them flush past but one copper dragged me out, threw me in front of him and shouted to get back. A friend from Twitter, Liam, was there. I think he told them to let go of me. I lied and said I had just come from work, and had gotten trapped. I wasn't anything to do with it. Please let me out. And they did. A second later I saw Liam and screamed and lied again and said he was my boyfriend and please to let him through.

They did.

I thought I failed the protest that night. But I suppose, I did actually help one person. I wrapped my arm around him as we walked away. That was the second time we'd met. We were both shaking.

My dad talking about stories

Throughout this audio Hannah writes something out on the back of a series of small wallet sized photographs "The moment when a feeling enters the body is political. This touch is political.- Adrienne Rich"

R: so if you look at the effect, at the outcomes of your protesting, which would you be more effective you think in terms of protesting, or entwining the issues amongst your work?

H: I think that they are all different aspects that it's worth covering in your resistance to ideas notions or actions. So I believe that if I were to make pieces of theatre or art that I am appealing to people's hearts, for

the most part. I am taking their body and asking them to put themselves in certain situations to empathise. I believe that by being a body on the street I am a symbol, I am turning myself into a symbol of somebody asking you to think or feel something, a symbol of something which is powerful, but not in a lot of ways; it won't change things. Like I've been thinking about this idea of whether I want to be a politician or I want to be an artist, and actually I think I'm more interested in empathy than I am in... in people's hearts than their minds. Because you're dealing with very small, what's the word, it means bit by bit...

R: incremental

H: incremental changes if you're working in government. And you can work all your life and change very small things which do make an actual difference, but that I think that the biggest lack at the moment is empathy, is the ability to understand someone else's point of view.[41] And I think the way that we get that is by telling and understanding, and listening to stories. I think that stories have been stolen by capitalism. I think that Hollywood in selling stories back to us, and it, it's only a one size fits all story. And so I think that we need stories now, more than we need the lawmakers.

R: I think you're right, and I think what you said earlier on about 'the bloody students again', you know, it's so and so, it's the EDL, it's the left wing loony left, you know the unions again; people can dismiss protests, particularly violent ones because it gives them a clear excuse to dismiss it. And I think the protests that do have some significance are those that don't end up in violence that cause, not sensational but cause visible

[41] Precisely!

presence, you have to take notice of them. But otherwise I think the only way that you can have a big impact if by changing people's views, by actually getting hold of their heart and squeezing it and saying; look at this. And I think as you say, it's having the story that triggers the emotion in the individual, which then says 'yeah, that's not right, we need to change this'. Because you won't get, there's too many pressures on people, and I think this is where capitalism wins through most of the time; there's too many pressures on people to stand out, to stand up, to say no, and I think by doing what your doing in terms of the stories, you know okay you can only get some people but that can make a big difference, than, you know, you as an individual amongst 200-300,000 people making a lot of noise down the street.

H: yeah

R: but I still respect you. You have a lot of courage in doing that.

My dad's respect means a lot to me. And I know that he is a fair man. My mum and dad bought a car together with the overtime that he earned policing the miners strikes, but they also donated the rest to pro-miner charities.

I'm proud of my dad. And I'm glad I had this conversation with him. His experiences, his point of view weren't much of a surprise to me, but some things were, he called me brave. And there was a trust in his respecting my decision to get myself into dangerous situations. And I heard him use the word 'capitalist' for the first time. This working class boy from a single parent family in Maidstone, who left school at 15, was perfect and eloquent on how change happens – whether through politics, the media, protest or theatre. It's all stories. It's about finding a way to listen, to try and understand, to cross the line and tread the space in between.

Together.

I haven't been to a national protest for a year and a bit, it's not that I don't want to, but my political energies have been directed a bit differently and to be honest, I've not been able to afford to get to London.

But I will go on more, and I will continue trying to find other ways to act. Because when I tell you that we're not the 'them' and the 'us' that you see in the media, I'm not saying we're special or good because of that, I'm telling you this is the life we live. This is real. This is me, and this is my dad.

I've got something I'd like to give you (after/on your way out/before we finish…)

Thank you.[42]

[42] I still find this a very moving piece. Thank you.

Songs for Breaking Britain

Introduction

In the late spring of 2013 I was invited by the awesome Laura Mugridge and Emma Frankland to take part in a residency with *The Campsite*, in a tent, on a campsite, in Cornwall. The offer was incredibly generous, and it's no mistake that the best work I've made has come out of no strings attached offers of support – first from Annabel, and secondly, here, from *The Campsite*. They urged me to not think of the week away as a time to produce something, but a time to be amongst 10-12 other artists, just thinking and reflecting and experimenting. I could only attend 3 of the days, but they made a huge difference to me, not least because just before then my friend John had died, and I was reeling a little. I remember talking to Emma, while she was bathing their little boy Jowan in a bucket, about duty of care. I was angry at myself for my first reaction to John's death being wanting to talk about him in a theatre piece, to talk about his impact on my approach to endurance sport, and for getting me to sign up to a marathon across the Lake District I was due to run in a few weeks. Emma listened carefully to me and then spoke about growing up in Cornwall and training to be a lifeguard. She said: you're taught something about 'duty of care' when you're taught how to save someone's life, you're told that you have a duty to use those skills if they can make a difference to someone in trouble. She related that idea of 'duty of care' to making art. That sometimes you have a duty of care to talk about things, if you have the craft that allows us to talk about those things together.

As part of those few days I also met Emma's brother, who co-ran *The Campsite*'s retreat: Keir Cooper. Keir is a jazz-rock musician and theatre maker, who primarily played guitar but was interested in getting into drumming. I spoke to him for a while about an idea I'd had for a few months, maybe half a year (I never remember where they start), of a punk show made up of songs written out of stories collected from people in the street. I'd already been developing my 'story collecting' practice for around 3-4 years at this point. Some of my first experimental works were audio pieces made out of stories collected from people on the internet, then work like *Dust* with Nikki Pugh, and *Northern Big Board*, made out of the stories of a community around a swimming pool in Shipley. Keir said he was pretty interested in being involved. And with a new sense of energy about the idea I posted on the UK DIY Punk Facebook group asking if anyone else would be interested in being involved. Sean Arnold, from a DIY pop punk band in Dundee called *Bonehouse* replied, and I met up with him when he was on tour at the Old Blue Last in the summer. We chatted, and he basically seemed up for... well, anything. Sean is like that.

So, I proposed the piece to Ovalhouse as part of their *You Might Also Like* season of seed commission double bills, and with success there, used that seed funding to support another larger ACE bid, featuring Theatre in the Mill, HUB in Leeds and ARC in Stockton again. Plus Alex Kelly on board as a designer, and with Hannah Jane Walker – an excellent poet and performer – agreeing to give me a crash course in spoken word and poetry, which I hoped would help me write lyrics.

I have been a part of the DIY punk/rock/math community for years now. Writing for 'zines, attending shows, buying records, owning more band tees than is reasonable for an average human, but I've never made music before. In fact, I consider myself wholly un-musical. At primary school I was one of those children who got told at some point they couldn't sing, and so mimed my way through a lot of the time

I could have actually used to practice. Genuinely one of the scariest things I can think of is Karaoke, so it felt kind of... bold, and DIY and everything that punk is about to me ('you too') to form a band of a guitarist who hadn't played drums before, a punk musician who had never even visited a theatre before, and me, a writer who had never made music, and was actually kind of scared of singing. This was the heart of the proposition – that we were all in a place of unusualness, and so, in turn, were the audience. Punk happening in a theatre, theatre happening in punk, and people in the street invited to confide in strangers. All of us slightly out of our comfort zones, all of us with a bit of space to think... new, in between things.

Presenting this show on paper is a lot harder than the other two. Because the performance is made up of the unusual collaborations, plus the process, plus the product. For that reasons I'm showing you a bit of all those things. First up, a description of how the story collecting worked. Then reflections from Sean and Keir on how they found the process and leading into how the music was made. Then the 'script' from the last time it was performed, in Hammersmith, London.

The heart of the idea of the show is that it is never 'finished', that every time it tours to a new venue it will collect new stories, and write a new song for the set list. A growing, ever changing thing, that reflects each place it visits. However, pitching to hard up venues to pay for even harder-up artists to turn up not just for one night, but also for 3 days including collecting, writing and rehearsal time as part of a tour is a really hard sell. It's not travelled as much as I would have liked it to, and for that reason *Songs for Breaking Britain* doesn't actually include any stories from Wales, or Scotland, or NI, or lots of place around England. It's on my list of things to do in 2017. Do it myself. Get it off the ground: a full UK tour.

Story collecting

It's a bit of an unwieldy phrase, that I mostly use to mean 'having conversations with people around a theme'. Very often this involves just being in public places and inviting strangers to offer me a moment of their time. I have sometimes tried to give out free tickets and lollipops in exchange for this kindness, but most often people seem happy enough to just have had a chance to chat. I work with what I call *questions everyone is an expert in*. Which is a way of constructing room for everyone to confidently approach complicated questions. It echoes artistic practices: I might be making a piece about 'Britishness' but as part of being an artist we unpack words and meanings and think around things in ways which are not a part of ordinary life and survival. The questions I write aim to do that unpacking for you. So I don't ask 'what does it mean to be British?', I first ask 'where would you say you're from?', then 'what does that mean to you?', then 'what are people like, from around here?' and then 'what makes you angry? Or happy? Or sad?' The questions circle the theme, and are always tied to the experience of the person answering. They are questions you can't answer 'wrongly' – you don't ask 'what's the best song' you ask 'what's your favourite song?'

The questions for this piece of work were written between the three of us, Sean, Keir and me. We tested them quite a lot, and kept on changing and sharing and rephrasing. We'd take a microphone, a clipboard and a pen, the questions, and ourselves out into the streets and ask people for a moment of their time. Recording our conversations with their permission. We would use the questions as leaping off points for storytelling, though, not as a survey. This method doesn't suit everyone, but Sean and Keir rose to the task magnificently.

There were more questions that this, eventually, but these are the central ones we normally started with:

Where would you say you are from?

What does that mean to you?

Do you like it here?

What /who inspires you?

What's the biggest injustice in Britain right now?

What does democracy/politics/community mean to you?

How much do you trust the papers/media?

What makes you angry?

Do you feel British? What does that mean to you?

Where do you feel happiest?

Do you like your job?

What do you care about?

What is important to you?

What's your favourite song?

Then the next step was to come back to the rehearsal room, to talk in turn about the people we met, to write up their names, their words, to discuss and work on the themes and characters and observations, and to try and turn those things into sounds and words and ideas that became songs.

Let's hear from Sean and Keir:

Sean Arnold:

I joined this process after seeing a post on Hannah's Facebook page asking for musicians who could possibly be interested in a new theatre project she was making. I had never done any theatre before and since leaving school

 I had focused mainly on touring and playing music and thought it was time to try and do something out of my comfort zone. I didn't really know what to expect from it, or even if anything would come out of it at all but before I knew it I was in was in London with Hannah and Keir not knowing what I had gotten myself into, but excited to see where it would end up.

I was nervous and felt like a charlatan tricking these well-meaning smart theatre makers into letting me into their theatre bubble. It was interesting to me to see how this world operated and felt that I learnt a lot from the different approach to making art.

One thing that really stuck me with me was at the beginning and end of every session we had preparing for the show we would take turns on just speaking our minds about absolutely anything, no matter how irrelevant or silly the thoughts were. I found that this unloading of worries and opening of hearts between us gave me confidence in what I was doing and really brought me closer to Hannah and Keir. It helped to make a much more creative atmosphere, where all ideas and approaches were valued and any criticisms we had were not taken personally but in the spirit of a shared goal of making the best content that we could all be proud of.

At first I thought I would only be involved with only the musical aspects of the show so when Hannah wanted me to go out and help with the story collecting I was a little bit scared of the prospect and doubtful of my ability to be of any use, but she did a great job of making me feel at ease and not feel any pressure to come up with anything good. I was there to try and do something different and I'm glad she pushed me because the story collecting turned out to be the most rewarding part of the project. The first few hours I nervously stood with my clipboard, anxiously smoking cigarettes and avoiding eye contact with people on the street, half approaching them then chickening out at the last minute, pretending I'm walking somewhere else. After a while this felt entirely pointless so I tried to gather some confidence and talk to someone. The first few conversations felt forced and one-sided, like I was just gathering information for a survey, not really listening or engaging in what they had to say. That wasn't what I was there to do. After going back in and hearing what Hannah and Keir had been up to and learning about the people they met I went back out into the street trying a different approach, not feeling the pressure to talk to as many people as possible but to try and relax and have at least one meaningful conversation with someone.

I remember meeting Irene in the walkway by the park just outside of Oval tube station. I remember the sun was shining and there was a fallen tree in the park because of a storm the night before. I remember the situation and the surroundings so well because my conversation with Irene really stuck with me. She was kind and fascinating and I could have talked to her for hours, it was exactly what I was looking for. She was the catalyst that made me stop worrying about my own fears of if my contribution to the show would be of any use because I realized that it really wasn't about me. I was there to give a voice to the people that I met and I was there to share their stories.

Making the music.

I really enjoyed the challenge of composing the music for this show. I had only ever met Hannah once briefly before and met Keir for the first time when we went for a meal to discuss the project so to be in a rehearsal room with them both with only 5 days to figure each other out and what type of show we were going to be making and come up with some original music felt like a lot of work. Ultimately I feel that because of this we added a real urgency to the music we made and the songs ended up with a more honest and imperfect tone to them. If we had had months to figure them out I reckon we would have lost that charm.

I tried to not come into the process with too much of an idea of how I wanted things to sound, but I knew that since the music would just be drums and guitar it would be more of a challenge to create something energetic and loud but with the right balance in not being the focus and to give Hannah's storytelling enough space to be heard properly. I wanted to jam and muck around with Keir as soon as possible so we could get a sense of how each other played and see the differences in our styles.

I come from a more thrashy abrasive way of making music whilst Keir seemed to have more of a jazz sensibility to him,

I was relieved after a few hours of mucking around together making noises that I think our styles complimented each other well. I knew that since we would be limited in what we could do instrumentation wise that working with dynamics and feel would be the key to making these songs.

I experimented with various guitar pedals to achieve this and gave myself a few different steps in volume and dirty tones with a reverb pedal to add a bit of atmosphere on the more quiet moments to fill it out. I tried various different open tunings to make my guitar sound fuller also.

Keir Cooper:

Joining the process of SFBB was instrumental for my arts practice in a few ways. I have spent many years writing for and alongside drums on rock/jazz outfits and even had  introduced myself in cavalier fashion to Hannah at a retreat in Cornwall as a performing monkey on drums (as I had been through a bout of performing an adaptation of Don Quijote where I break into drum and bass on a kit in costume). Aside from this experience, I had never found a need (though the desire was always there) to learn and play drums. This process lead me to devote some time to practicing and thinking about drums, and off the back, I even become a drummer for an internationally touring band, playing drums at Field Day and festivals in Madrid – it is now part of my practice.

But that is now. Going back to the beginning, I really had to work to find a method of contributing music that could pass as acceptable composition and find a language where a punk guitarist and a trepid vocalist on her fist foray into bands could forge some coherent material. Sometimes I felt like I was translating between the two other makers in some hinterland between rock writing vernacular and theatre making vernacular. Sometimes I found that it was I who was lost in the discussion as I have found that my home turf, the place I grew up with musically – talking in rock tongues now leaves me a little more confused than bringing in language from different musical canons. From the work I do elsewhere, I find myself between worlds – with a half learned understanding of certain vocabularies and here – using a half remembered understand of speaking around the language – D.I.Y and non-academy.

I expected the process to be more straightforward (musically). I thought we'd have more given time to write the work and, truthfully, I had no expectations of the community verbatim stuff. This was new – I'd never seen any and never made any. It was exhilarating to speak with strangers – I love an excuse to make a momentary connection with people, but it felt less like art that I am used to and more like other work. This was not totally unwanted and had its own aesthetic and enjoyment. Except sometimes people were horrendous with their views and when it was too goddamn cold. Then we'd get back to a bubble of making – comfort and warmth.

The music:

My long-term collaborator Oliver came to see the piece in Hammersmith. After the performance I explained that the songs had been composed sometimes in as little as half a day – his approach to the pieces changed and he declared that this should've been known earlier as it was THIS that was the interesting and relevant component in the work. Hearing the songs with a different critical ear than work that has been rehearsed and crafted over months on end. This is about the here and now. A visceral response to a place, a time, connections and was actually about sketching in pen not pencil. This is the offer and the audience need to know this to be expected to read the work with the appropriate context. And then it becomes a bit of a skill too. The short turnaround turns that element into another instrument – the tool of quick decisions and songcraft.

Something that was essential to the process was having quick reference points to navigate by. We drew up an influence playlist so that at any given point if we were bereft of inspiration we could go back to history and springboard back into making.

Particular influences that can be heard and traced pretty nakedly include:

Jonny Greenwood – There Will Be Blood – Prospectors Arrive.
Enablers
Tool – Laturalus (the song).
The Monkeys / Wildhearts / McFly[43]

As we are a fairground mirror of our influences, it's perhaps quicker and more practical to do this consciously than to rely on the personal subconscious assimilation of influences that make up personal taste – just as informed by music history as the former.

The other thing I've learned about working with Sean particularly is that some musicians love to rehearse loud. I feel too fragile for this, I'd much rather rehearse at 1/3 volume while writing then crank it up at the end. My ears tire quickly, and it's really difficult to think. I love him dearly and also have no idea how anyone can sustain that much auditory intensity. His opening tuning techniques and regular capo usage really

---

[43] Because I can't resist adding my own in, these are some of the bands I sent Sean and Keir: *La Dispute; ManBearPig; Captain, We're Sinking; Kate Tempest; Peter Wyeth; The Middle Ones; Mahria; Carson Wells; The Wild; Adequate Seven; The Front Bottoms; Toe; Olympians.*

brought a specific and enlivened broad tone to the songs and the show and have been borrow in my own guitar practice since.

For an example of how we worked together, take the Bradford song: this came about from Sean and I trying to find a big funky riff that glitches in time and pulls and stretches things in an interesting way. I sketched out a rhythm and taught it to Sean and we tried to make a biff riffing metal thing. After we'd conducted the interviews and found that the content didn't require such a visceral bold frame, we made a ballad and reimagined the rhythms oscillating between guitar and drums in various incantations of the verses. Doing an isorhythmic pattern where the material met anew at each given point in time. In short, we made a ballad and gave it a subtly rhythmic sheen of intricacy that provides the interest once the melodic ideas are established.

Hannah:

Back with me again. One last thing to add to the discussion of song making is that as part of this I was learning to write lyrics, perform to and with rhythms, and listen to music well enough so that I knew where and how to come in. For some people these things are second nature, but for me, this part of the process was difficult and at once elating and frustrating. Hannah Jane Walker's two-day workshop with me on poetry was absolutely instrumental in shaping my writing for this, and continues to influence me. I very often run workshops sharing some of the tools she gave me because they are so useful. Hannah Jane Walker also came to the first work in progress of the show at Ovalhouse in the Autumn of 2013, and reflected that for the words to be really heard – we were asking the audience to listen – we needed to find a new space, a space between that wasn't the punk, and that wasn't the theatre or spoken word, an in between space where the words sometimes rebelled against the rhythm to find their own space, and sometimes bubbled up as part of the song. This was an important, astute and highly valuable observation.

And then, in Stockton, the boys finally got me singing. As part of the 'No Song' there was a chorus which Sean originally sang, but that in its current version, I sing with him. By Bradford, we made and composed a song which I am particularly fond of, and join in an actual harmony with, I think that song is one of the most beautiful things I have ever been a part of making. It is in that moment, where some people coming together produce something none of them could have imagined, it's there that we find the heart of this show.

A final note: on the beautiful design and staging of Alexander Kelly. He came in during the final week of four, and he immediately and perfectly understood the show. He knew that it was about all of us being in a room together, and being so unusually. He knew that we needed to be honest about all of the things that we had to cut, that didn't make it, but that were also what the piece was built on. He knew it needed to feel DIY: rough, and ready. That it needed to work in low-tech spaces. And to allow room for the energy of the sounds and ideas and song. How he did that is pictured and explained in detail below. But simply put: we covered a 3m circle with A4 and A3 sheets of all of our handwriting, listing both the questions we asked and the names of every person we spoke to. My script was always in hand because the show would be re-written every time we performed it, and Alex printed this script on a rich yellow gold paper colour. As I finished pages I let them fall to the floor. We performed in the centre of the audience, in a circle to one another, and out. I would move around and talk to people. Sean and Keir would also look up and out and tell stories. At the end of the performance, we put our instruments down and leave, as a selection of the people we talk to speak from a collage of their recordings. That is how it ends.

Songs For Breaking Britain

Set Design and LX notes

For use in conjunction with 'Generic Set Diagram'

A Draw/mark out/imagine an approximately 3 metre diameter circle which will be the central performance area.

B Lay out the paper 'set lists' of questions and names. These should roughly line up top-towards-the-centre, bottom-towards-the-edge of the circle, rather than scattered at random. They don't need to completely 'wallpaper' the floor, a few gaps between them are fine.

Depending on the surface of the floor, you may need to spray mount the sheets to the floor – particularly where Hannah dances. If the bottom few big sheets have an 'X' of spray mount on them, then the ones above should be fine with the same. In areas where Hannah doesn't dance, you proably don't need to stick it down.

As spray mount is adjustable, hopefully some of the sheets will be re-usable… So use as much as you need so there are no dancing injuries.

C Position the Drums rug, Guitar position and vocal position on top of the white sheets.

<u>Lighting positions, in order of priority (in the event that LX is limited):</u>

D Three parcans positioned in the gaps between perfomers; exact position will depend on height of grid; focussed on the paper to draw people in; bounced light from the white paper will light the performers faces. This might be enough in some spaces.

E Three profiles or fresnels, shallower angle than the parcans, to pick out each performer. (If LX stock available, splitting each of these into pairs to make them more side-on is an option.)

F Three fresnels to provide back light to each performer.

Around this basic set up, be flexible to make it work in each space.

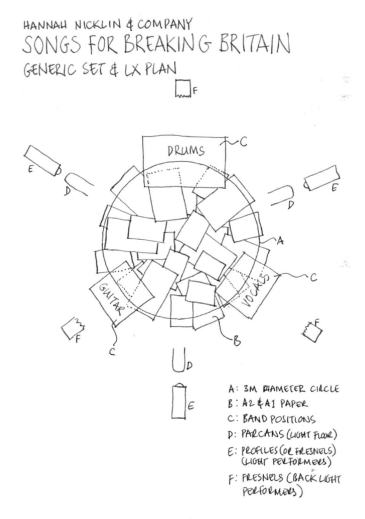

HANNAH NICKLIN & COMPANY
SONGS FOR BREAKING BRITAIN
GENERIC SET & LX PLAN

DRUMS

GUITAR

VOCALS

A: 3M DIAMETER CIRCLE
B: A2 & A1 PAPER
C: BAND POSITIONS
D: PARCANS (LIGHT FLOOR)
E: PROFILES (OR FRESNELS) (LIGHT PERFORMERS)
F: FRESNELS (BACK LIGHT PERFORMERS)

Songs for Breaking Britain

Hannah, Sean and Keir walk on, pick up their instruments

Hannah: Hello. This is Sean, This is Keir, I'm Hannah. And This is *Songs for Breaking Britain*

DRUMS
This is a drilling, rhythmic roll call of a song. The drums are a marching pace, and each name falls into the rhythm. Every name we've spoken to in that place is mentioned in the Name Song, plus some from previous places.

THE NAME SONG

Roshina
Isobel
Rebecca
Francesca
Irene
Gabriel
Joyce, walking, "they don't care, they don't care about us" not me, not me, maybe whitey, not me

Nina
Josie
Ben
James
Roberto
Jordy
Lawrence with two lifeboat pins carefully affixed both lapel and tie.

Manbir
Maja (maya)
Kay
Austeja (austere)
Dean Certes
Gladys

Sikander – with a knife scar on the back of his head, who won't be happy until he's in heaven

Karen
Jawad Ahmed
Julia and Janaed
Sue
Lola
The iraqi man who didn't want to go by his real name, so chose 'Mr Human'

Frederick
Waqas
Paul
Lou
Terry
Barbara
Anastaios
Abdullah
Mickey, Mickey who had been clean for 9 months now. Mickey, whose grandkids had seen him clean for the first time.

The song changes and becomes meandering

The man who spent the whole conversation unlocking his bike.
The British hindu convert who hated british culture
Harry McCallister who said retirement is the best thing that ever happened to him,
Louis, who said he was tired of being a victim of racial profiling
Khan, who talked about peace in your heart and peace in your head.
Two unison workers dressed as the grim reaper and Edward scissorhands.
And the life long friends, who said 'mate, everyone round here is on the brown,'

SONGS FOR BREAKING BRITAIN

The song begins to build

olive skin and freckles
White streaks in a black beard
heavy gold earrings
bright amber brown eyes.

Eton Rifles by the Jam
A Perfect Day by Lou Reed
When two worlds drift apart
Thrift Shop by Mackelmore

Hands held long after handshakes finished.
Gilt earrings with three pearls
Light brown skin,
Strong black glasses
A Flyaway fringe

Meshuggah
Paramore
Reggae played through a mobile phone
Elvis Presley
Keaton Henson
Martin Garrix
William Blake's Jerusalem
Chaka Khan.

Crescendo, then a pause, this is said in silence

And the boy-nearly man who stood in front of his mates and
described to me what it was like to be in prison

The song breaks, it plays out loud and heavy.

We've been out in the streets of 3 cities, London, Stockton on
Tees, and Bradford.

Sean: Streets Description

Sean improvises these each time, beginning with the text in bold

You go down the street
And you notice there's a light brown dull colour of the buildings
The bare trees with too much mud
And the smell of cigarette smoke

You go down another street
And you notice the fallen branches on the floor that joggers are stepping around
You notice people from young to old all mixing walking past each other
And the big wide expansive park which you can't get in because of the locked gate

You go down another street
And you notice the big expanse of concrete and one or two people dotted around walking across
You notice how bare it is
You notice how everyone doesn't want to be there, is just trying to get to where they're going.

You go down another street
You notice 1 (specific to the new place)
You notice 2 (specific to the new place)
You notice 3 (specific to the new place)

Hannah: We've been out into the streets of 3 cities. And we've been asking people to talk to us.

Before we tell you more about the people we met in all 3 places though – one thing all of them had in common was that they all contained people who didn't want to talk to us.

Londoners dismissed us with a kind of weary lack of surprise. People in Stockton seemed to defend themselves against the idea you must want to take something from them.

And in Bradford, it seemed much rarer to see women walking alone, and there were a lot of people rushing for trains.

So we wrote a song for them. The people who didn't make the sample. The 'no's. The ones we'll never know anything about.

E B E A B E *(tuning note)*

THE NO SONG

Sean and Keir begin a poppy punk feeling song with a catchy riff. Keir cues Hannah who speaks the following

"We have nothing to say"
they said
in different voices, through different eyes
under heavy fringes, stooped shoulders
curls that yearned for the sky

"sorry mate no thanks"
"what are you selling?"
"Who's paying for this?"
"what do you mean you're making theatre?"

A shift in the music, it tumbles over into a chorus, sung by all three

Couples walking, eyes evade
Their heads buried in their screens
Earbuds pressed back into place
Changing paths to not be seen.

Straight in, speaking:

We asked: "Where are you from"
and got looks hung with suspicion,
Minds searching after the hook –
The bit where we would try and get them to sign up for something.

"I'm sorry, I'm sorry, I need to be at work"
"I'm not selling anything, I'm not raising for a charity-"
these words tumbled down over ears blocked with getting elsewhere.

Couples walking, eyes evade
Their heads buried in their screens

Earbuds pressed back into place
Changing paths to not be seen.

"I'm sorry I don't speak english" a bright rose red headscarf, dark eyeliner, two buggies.

A woman who said she couldn't stop but "I could tell you stories, I could write them down, my friends say so, better than Thelma and Louise"

A G4S man obscured by his bullet proof vest, smiling a sad 'no sorry'

And a man who – when Sean explained that 3 of us were making some theatre – stormed off saying "I thought this was something proper"

Couples walking, eyes evade
Their heads buried in their screens
Earbuds pressed back into place
Changing paths to not be seen.
x lots.
End of song.

You go to each city you visit with a set of expectations. And each time, with each person they are gently confounded.

Hannah: Steve

Steve was a construction worker I spoke to in Bradford – I had an immediate affinity for him because he looked a lot like my uncle – he had the same soft demeanour of a strong man, and also because my uncle is a Yorkshireman called Steve.

Most of his answers to the questions were pretty standard – he liked his work, he had strong views about patriotism and how it's connected to military service and mentioned how both his granddad and dad had died of military wounds.

And he chatted a bit about how he had no problem with foreigners but he did feel like they effected how difficult it was for him to get work, and he was probably right.

I would never have found out the thing that surprised me about Steve if I hadn't had made up a really stupid new question. Something about him made me think "shepherd".

So I asked him 'if you lived 200 years ago what do you think you'd do"? He didn't really know how to answer this, deservedly, but somehow it led on to a conversation about his upbringing, and he mentioned poetry and painting he did with his mum.

I asked what kind of painting and poetry and he said that actually, he still painted –

where he couldn't before answer the question 'what inspires you' suddenly he was talking about the time, a few years ago, he started collecting old cupboard doors out of skips, painting them with sky, and glueing military aircraft cut out of old magazines to them.

And then he thought 'well why not have a go at painting them'.

His sister who went to college helped him, gave him tips about light and shade and thinking about where the sun was in them.

And now he paints lots of things. He has hundreds. Everything except portraits. He said he's thinking about putting them on eBay so people can see them.

The stories we tell ourselves about each other are not big enough.

The next song is the one we wrote for Bradford. The story, if I'm honest, that I know about Bradford, is race tensions. Is George Galloway, riots, is the surging Yorkshire BNP membership. But that tension is not what we heard. Mostly.

Race and ethnicity did come up – Louis who said when he goes to Leeds to gigs he's always pulled over by the police when his white friends aren't.

Sikunder, who said injustice was "Pakis getting pulled over by cops every minute, racial abuse" – but a lot of people from many backgrounds talked about how proud they were to be from Bradford, the ease they have with dual, multi, or personal nationalities, they felt really... together.

And also – Bradford was always talked about in terms of the wider county – the dales were always on the edge of people's minds.

This song is named after a phrase we heard again and again, people said they were "Bradford born and bred".

Born and Bred

This song is careful and quiet and beautiful, the guitar picks out a rhythm that dances around drumming that is subtle and complicated. Hannah is cued after a long introduction. Spoken:

Somewhere on the edge of Bradford this morning a girl called Sophie woke up.
She did all the normal morning things, as usual she's in no rush.
Early 20s, she spoke to Keir who described her as having ginger eyes,
he said she sounded wise.

Her mother is Ukrainian,
but when Sophie speaks there is a weight to her words.
thick with dropped consonants,
Bradford through and through
She finishes her breakfast, pulls on a blue waterproof coat,
leaves the house.

She only has to walk around the corner to find it -
it's just a field, one like most people could think of
a patch of trees in the middle, quite big.
She's gone there every day since she was young - happy, sad,
even just for a few minutes.
and she sits there now, together looking over Bradford.

Keir and Sean sing:

old mills, bittersweet
empty cathedrals to industry
hawthorn describing
ragged boundaries
hills of sandy loam,
breathless skies,
dark cream-black stone.

cued:

In the city Austeja (*pron: Austere*) is walking for her train under
the shadow of the clock tower,
she thinks sometimes that the architecture of Bradford's old
buildings feel like Romania -
her thoughts are sometimes from England, sometimes from
Lithuania.
'Here', she will tell us, 'all mixes'.

Steve Kettlewell's name goes back to the 17th century.
He describes the noise of a rebounding spring that always
brings him back to this city.
Steve is 59, a construction worker, unemployed
Describes how, aged 17, he used to cry each time he had to
leave for his apprenticeship.

He says "born and bred in Bradford,
there's something you just love about the place,
the country, the Dales -
the accent as well.
I'm happiest here - in my home town -
wherever I go I always come back -
it's like being on a coiled spring -
anyone who was born in Bradford -
something in their blood",
it attracts, like a magnet.

Keir and Sean sing:

old mills, bittersweet
empty cathedrals to industry
hawthorn describing
ragged boundaries
hills of sandy loam,
breathless skies,
dark cream-black stone.

Julia and Janaed, Pakistani British and Bengali Irish,
out for the first time since their Sienna was born

They are some of the few people who come up to us and ask
to be interviewed,
They look slightly dazed, move like they're connected
completing each other's sentences
she says "Polish, Slovakian, Italian"
he says "we're all the same, all Bradford'

Sophie sighs. Now at work, but some part of her still looks over
the city from a distance,
the dark Cliffe Wood stone, mined centuries ago from a local
quarry on Bolton Road.

Hannah joins in singing this time:

old mills, bittersweet
empty cathedrals to industry
hawthorn describing
ragged boundaries
hills of sandy loam,
breathless skies,
dark cream-black stone.

Fahard Ali, in a mustard coloured flat cap wearing darkened
glasses describes Britishness as a language spoken:
his energetic movements form words under a fast sky
"being British is about the natural dominion of the island and
coast and sea,
the topography, the people, the struggles we've gone through,
the literature, the architecture -
Charles Barry, Lincoln cathedral -
it's not a singularity, it's a laminated effect -
and let's not forget it's been 100 years since the beginning of
the first world war -
we're also a product of that -
we came out poorer, lost 3 generations of men,
had to rebuild ourselves;
empire and the loss of empire,

the joining up of people through the commonwealth.
You can be British if you've lived here four hours
or if you've been here all your life -
it's about how you relate to it, how you contribute.
I'm from Yorkshire, god's own country."

Home.

Hannah jokes about how that is genuinely verbatim. A man genuinely said all those things. It was a magnificent thing to behold.

Keir: My favourite question to ask

My favourite question to ask was "what is your favourite song?"
it always elicited the best response

Improvised:

- **people's reactions** *Keir talks about how people responded, it was always a lovely conversation to have*
- **different to other questions because** *It was the question that most summed up the idea of 'questions everyone is an expert in'*
- **important because** *it also summed up the show, and the person you were talking to – it gave you a sense of time, place, background, and also of the idea that we build ourselves through our culture*
- **political because** *the political is personal, the personal is political.*

Hannah: Stockton is a small market town near Middlesbrough.

Unemployment, according to the Tees Valley Unlimited 2013 report is nearly double that of Great Britain. We got difficult stories in both London and Bradford but there was such a wide variation of themes in those places – in Stockton the 'biggest injustice' always came back to the same two things unemployment – and to immigration.

This song is called 'From Here'.

FROM HERE.

This song is loud and angry and instant. It features screaming and heavy angular sounds.

Screamed:
I'm proud
I'm proud I live here

Spoken: "I just try to be open with people. Not judgmental."

Screamed:
Our nation
defined by acceptance

Spoken: "Because that's what people do to me, and I don't like it"

Screamed:
The army
changed my perspective

Spoken: The army changed the way I thought - gave me a *bigger* perspective.

Screamed:
No longer
a British country.

Spoken: I *can* understand why people would want to come here.

Screamed:
I'm proud
I'm proud I live here
Our nation
defined by acceptance

The army
changed my perspective

No longer
a British country.

/ / / / /

The music changes here, becomes heavy and low

Long thin scar on the right side of his face
'me, I'm just out of the army mate'
home is friends he's known all his life
'Cousin's a sniper, I was yorks regiment'

Shoulder height, fine light blue scarf covering
her head, 'Naz' with a zed. Voice hard to sort
from the noise of the streets. Black eyeliner
pencil drawn - proud - proud to be British.

British is being born here - if you're born here you're British
The town was never like this, then they started coming
shops closing down, NHS failing
close the borders, close the borders.

Naz walked, weighed her words. Stockton,
to her, was multicultural, Britishness; tolerance.
Then she hesitated. Except around the time
of the 7/7 bombings, then, then it was difficult.

/ / / / /

He walked a street being torn up. Construction
sounds reverberating beneath us.
He stood opposite boarded up shops, jobless
He said he understood though, He said he understood it.

She talked as we walked, disappearing into
a thick black coat. She spoke about the insults
her children suffered, how she feels like
she has to represent all Muslims.

/ / / / /

Screamed:
I'm proud
I'm proud I live here
Our nation
defined by acceptance

The army
changed my perspective
No longer
a British country.

/ / / / /

The music changes again

Never as simple as we are all encouraged to think
He had compassion, but also tearing, choking
poverty. He doesn't have nothing, he doesn't have much,
we like stories that tell us it's them not us.

She said she was not the person they think - her
accent dripping the flat edged vowels of the north east
They look at her and see one thing. Her
mouth shaped the words "it's hard to be human, isn't it?"

/ / / / /

I'm proud
I'm proud I live here

"I just try to be open with people. Not judgmental."

Our nation
defined by acceptance

"Because that's what people do to me, and I don't like it"

The army
changed my perspective

> *The army changed the way I thought – gave me a bigger perspective.*

I'm proud
I'm proud I live here

> *End of music*

We've been into London twice. But London is not really one place, everyone knows that. Much more so than any other city in the country, it's a billion places all at once. We went to South London in February, and last weekend we were talking to people in Hammersmith. I'd like to give you a well-thought out reason about wanting to compare West London to South London but mostly it's because both of these theatres wanted to book us. Both Londons felt different. But we were in different kinds of places; in South London we were on a busy road, next to a large housing estate. Here, we were just outside the theatre, in this square, by the fountains and the shops. In South London there were people who lived where we collected stories, in Hammersmith, outside the Lyric, it was more of a place of crossing, a collection of noise and meeting, more of a patchwork.

City Song

2 x 8 bar intro.

Outside the William Morris,
now a wetherspoons
pigeons bathe ragged in the fountain
cities of stone that
mould us in return

Architecture guiding the eye
fountains like an eddy
in the flow of people
Julian - stylish but supicious
says "be careful with my words"
while Ed watches his children play.
A toddler screams and hurtles at a bird

Bridge, then
4 x 8 intro again

The city is a blanket
the city is a rhythm
wrapped tight
smothering warm
seams pull and stretch
orange light swims
playing/hide/and/seek
pause
with missed horizons

// leave it 4 bars

Jane demolishes Brentford High Street in her mind
Keith hisses "London Overspill"
Gemma stages a retreat
to Richmond Park on her bike
Irene's eyes open wide with
the skies of North West Scotland

While a missing persons poster
stares out at us from the lampposts

A couple stand in public,
hand on his chest,
his arms outstretched,
tears stain her face.

LOUD BIT
//
space, 1 chord x2
//

"I'm British, my children were born here".
But I also come from Rotterdam,
India, Dublin, Nigeria.
"We're worried about immigration"
They gesture to inkjetted signs
'Missing: Alice'.

A woman carefully sorts through the bins
Cradling a discarded Costa packet
Ambika says
"I shouldn't feel ashamed for the money that I earn,"
"We all have responsibilities"

Sunlight reflects off a passing bus
A stranger rushes up
handing back the oyster card dropped.

Ijabo. A nurse,
says the world is getting scarier,
she intervened in an attack on a woman a year earlier
Her headscarf bright and floral
Held in place with a single pin
She says "that night my heart stopped".

LOUD bit

The city is a blanket
The city is a rhythm
Wrapped tight
smothering warm
seams pull and stretch
orange light swims
playing hide and seek
with missed horizons

People in different cities walk at different speeds
outside the William Morris,
now a Wetherspoons
"you used to be able to drive right through here"
pigeons bathe ragged in the fountain
cities built of stone that
mould us in return
cities built of stone that
mould us in return

Sean: John

Here Sean improvises telling the story about John, a man he met in Stockton, and someone who really affected Sean. John is a homeless man, who lost his home because he was in a coma when he should have been at a Job Centre appointment. He was sanctioned, and in the loss of JSA, was forced onto the streets.

- In Stockton I met John
- John looked like
- His demeanour
- The story
- It made me feel sad that he didn't have any friends and family looking out for him
- It made me angry that the job centre...
- Everyone should have someone looking out for them

Keir: Elaine

Here Keir does a similar improvisation about the person who stood out to him the most.

I remember speaking with a woman called Elaine
She was aged 50 or 60
I found her standing outside a building smoking a cigarette
    I remember Elaine had
white yellow skin, but in an interesting way, not a weird one
she was pretty in her own way
She was wearing an old red fleece
    I remember I asked directions for a music shop
she seemed friendly
so I asked if I could ask the questions for this show
    I remember she said yes
I began, then I got to "who or what inspires you"
She said 'nothing'
I remember thinking 'ah.'
You get answers like that sometime,
People think they're doing you a favour by answering quickly

I thought 'it's my responsibility to probe further, you don't mean nothing.'

OK

"you must have some dreams"

I remember her going – no I'm sorry, they're gone, my husband and my mother died around the same time so now my dreams aren't possible

I remember feeling a sense of shame of bringing up a conversation that wasn't intended.

So I remember trying to finish, but she wanted to continue

So I tried to make it as short as possible

I remember I asked her what the biggest injustice

And she said 'having to work'

And I think I understood what she meant by that

I remember I thanked her for her time

I remember she left

I remember as she walked away

I noticed for the first time it said WILCO in big white letters across her back

There was something quite tragic about how she was stamped with that

The company owned her

I remember Elaine because she cried. I didn't mean for that to happen.

Hannah: This our song from South London.

The Work Song

A driving, irresistible drum rhythm pushes this song along. It is hard work to perform, and hard work to watch Keir repeat the rhythm over and over and over.

Terry.
Terry was a big guy, shaved head, early 40s, white,
proper south London lad in a blue tracksuit,
a solid strut of a walk.
He was, it turned out, gentle and properly smiley.
Terry said "South London is…. Working class, family roots, proud of our community,
hard working people"

Hard working. We can't escape our history. And the fact is, in Britain, we struggle a bit with how tangled up our worth is with the work we do.

A protestant work ethic hangover

Josie said welfare is Britain's biggest strength and weakness.
Ben bemoaned the taxes "wasted on people who don't want to work".

While Mickey told me that David Cameron can't understand, how could he? 12 million in the bank, two homes "the way they've done the cuts is really slaughtering people."

3 separate individuals said the biggest injustice in Britain today is the bedroom tax.

I slightly anxiously approach a man in his van,
window down,
black Nike cap high on his forehead,
stabbing at his phone.
I ask if he has 5 minutes to tell me a story.

He says his favourite day of the week is Monday.
He works with water,
and he loves it,
his company is small, not worried about targets,
he loves the fact that they provide something that "not one
living thing on this earth could do without".
A single father.
A hard worker.
Proud.

It's a tough subject. Work.
So tied up in our worth and this left over protestant idea that if
we don't have it we're worth less.
That it makes you worth less if you can't,
sapping something significant of you if you feel like you're not
living up to your potential.
It can make you feel lost.
It can make you feel lost.
Nothing to do,
or turning around and looking back at 50 years
and now wondering what this is,
this time,
this space,
this body
with no purpose.

IRENE

*There is a break in the guitar as Sean tells us about Irene, who he met,
who had worked all of her life, several jobs to bring up her daughters.*

It's a tough subject.
Work.
So tied up in our worth
and this left over protestant idea that if we don't have it we're
worth less.
It can make you feel lost.
It can make you feel lost.

Nothing to do, or turning around
and looking back at 50 years
and now wondering what this is,
this time,
this space,
this body
with no purpose.

(K reduces the drumming)

And then there was Curtis, who is a youth worker,
said his job is not the greatest pay,
but it is the greatest reward.
Late 20s, fine black skin,
a full beard in tight curls,
broad.
He spoke to Keir
in a baritone with warmth and an easy smile
"not the greatest pay, but the greatest reward".

And to me,
a tall man with an identity card on a lanyard tucked into his
jumper,
Edinburgh accent eroded by 20 years of cosmopolitan living
– his word –
said simply
"Without love it's just struggle
struggle
struggle."

Hannah: worries

I am a worrier.

I worry that Sean who is not very practised at trains – he tends to use the Megabus – will get on the wrong train some day we have to perform this and end up in Cardiff instead of Norwich

I worry that I will miss a cue. Because I don't understand music that brilliantly these guys have a few moments where they cue me and I worry that they will forget and I will be left waiting and not sure how to come in without ruining it.

I worry that I might slip over on one of these pieces of paper and knock myself out.

I worry that the open questions we ask people sometimes leave them vulnerable

I worry that the process requires us to listen to, to hold the words of sometimes vulnerable people, and that sometimes they weigh too much.

I worry that because this show is drawn from a sample of people, it might look like an experiment and that people might try to draw conclusions from it, that I might try and conclude it, when it shouldn't. It should just be some stories.

Hannah: The most important thing for me about the show

This show begins and ends with listening.
We listen to some strangers in the street then we pass it on, put it into some songs, and you listen to them.
Stories exist because people listen to them.
Listening says 'that is an important thing'
'I hear it.' 'You are important. I hear you'
Stories are the way we tell ourselves about each other.
They are how we teach our children
Stories work with the basic unit – person.
Stories are political
Stories begin and end with listening.

> *An edit of the voices of the people we spoke to on the street*
> *begins. Some funny, some sad, some thoughtful.*
> *Hannah Sean and Keir leave the performance area.*

End.

Equations for a Moving Body

Introduction

If you read the introduction to *Songs for Breaking Britain*, you'll have spotted one of the beginnings to this piece. Actually it has three. The first is talking to Emma Frankland about duties of care, about what I should do with my urge to talk about my the death of my friend John. Then, when I left that retreat, a month or so after, I saw another Hatch: Nottingham scratch event looking for short pieces of work

to exhibit. So for that I made a piece called *Deadtime*.[44] It was a one-on-one performance in a little cubbyhole. The piece was recorded as audio, an audience member would come in, I'd welcome them, fit them with headphones, check they were ok, and the story would begin. The room was lit only with the light of a projector, and as the audio begins, I (in a white top) become the screen. As the story is told,

[44] The title drawing on the Situationist International influenced May 1968 graffiti'd phrase "Live Without Dead Time".

I live-Google and play through the things the story mentions: video of sitting on buses, tracing a route I ran with John in Loughborough across Google Maps, playing *Super Hexagon*, an animation of the time it takes for several billion trades to be made on the stock exchange.

It was a short 20 minute piece about losing a friend, and how we think about time, how we occupy the space in our heads and the wholeness of our bodies.

A little later, in the spring of 2014, I was walking with my friend, amateur trampolinist, and also arts-type-person Rajni Shah. Rajni is a very wise person, she always takes time and care with the conversations you have with her, and I really value the time we get to walk and talk together. At this point we were walking around Crystal Palace Park, home to one of my favourite swimming pools.[45] I was training for the 70.3 mile/113km middle distance triathlon, the *Cotswold 113* around then, and I distinctly remember saying to Rajni, while we got lost in the CPP maze "I just wish someone would pay me to do sport for a living". Rajni paused, and then with that particular clarity she has, said "why don't you then? Make a show about it?"

I laughed at first. And then I thought. I saw suddenly how *Deadtime* was also piece about the experience of the mind and body during sport, which related to my friend John, which related to my thoughts around why I had decided to do an Ironman[46] (or 'full distance') triathlon.

The third beginning for the show was entering the idea (still called *Ironman* at this point) to *Title Pending*, a competition for

---

[45] After Loughborough University, and the Edinburgh Commie.

[46] Ironman is the brand but it's really become synonymous with the distance, so I often use this as shorthand, knowing it's not 100% correct. I actually, in the end, signed up to the Outlaw, which is the same full-distance, but not an Ironman branded event. This I regret only because it makes the whole thing so damn complicated to explain each time.

substantial support (financial, mentoring, technical, space) to begin work on a new piece of theatre. If nothing else my work is an advert for how vital the offering of money, time, expertise and space is in the arts community. I won the *Title Pending Award 2014*, and with the support of Northern Stage, and that of Northumbria University, ARC Stockton, Camden People's Theatre (CPT) in London, and eventually Theatre Studio at Sheffield University and Carriageworks in Leeds I put in two bids to the Arts Council, and The Wellcome Trust, for an ambitious project that involved investing in a coach, training gear, research, time to train, as well as the making of the show. I worked with Alex Kelly of Third Angel again, and this time our collaboration was much more balanced, I was more experienced, and we knew one another as makers. The making process was often interrupted by my training (it was designed to be) and throughout the 6 months of time I did between 8 and 16 hours of swimming, cycling and running a week, worked with Simon Ward, a triathlon coach, interview sports scientists and psychologists and Alex and I worked on finding out what the story was.

The process was designed around the *Outlaw*. The full distance triathlon I eventually signed up to, which happened on the 26th July 2015. We made most of the show *before* I attempted the *Outlaw*, and then with one day to rest, finished the material in the week following. I mostly remember not being able to walk for more than 15 minutes without feeling dizzy, having to leave rehearsals early because I was so drained. At the work in progress showing I downed a Coke (a thing I'd never normally drink) just to hold my glycogen levels together long enough to tell the story. Alex remembers it differently though. Apart from the initial two days after, he said I "was glowing".

Then, with all the material completed, in October, we had a week in Sheffield and Leeds, finding the shape and structure of the story.

A note on the process and the staging from Alexander Kelly:

One of the really interesting things for me about this process was how the temporal nature of it changes – each time we worked on it we were in a different place in time in relation to the event that the show is (partly) about. Back in February we were a long way off. It still felt almost hypothetical (to me at least). Hannah got her training schedule from her coach during that fortnight at Northern Stage, so the Outlaw was still something Hannah was going to train to do. One of my favourite pieces of material from that stage in the process was Hannah talking about imagining crossing the line. "I don't see my self crawling," she would say, "when I picture it, I am running over the line."

For the fortnight at ARC, the Outlaw Triathlon was something that Hannah was training to do. On a practical level it impacted on our process more (though of course the training is process, in this instance). She trained each morning and we talked and researched and made the show in the afternoons and evenings.

Thematically though, it shifted our relationship with the science, and the research, and the narrative. If Hannah got injured[47] it could affect her final performance. We were at the last stage where a serious injury is recoverable from. Early on in the process my assumption was that Hannah would complete the triathlon. As I found out more about the science of endurance sport, more about the world of triathlon (at the time I was reading Chrissie Wellington's *A Life Without Limits* – which I really liked), the more I discovered about what else can go wrong – other than not being fit enough.

---

[47] I did actually take a reasonably bad tumble on a 30 minute run off a 5 hour bike ride during that week, and was limping for a few days.

Put bluntly, I realised it was not a given that Hannah would cross the finish line. So, whilst this probably sounds obvious, we didn't yet know, in Stockton, how the narrative we were telling would finish.

**

On our previous collaboration *A Conversation With My Father*, the form of the piece was already set when I came on board; my job was to help Hannah expand on the 25 minutes she already had – to attach building blocks of material to the existing core of the show.

With *Equations for a Moving Body*, the project was less established, formally. We had talked about the ideas behind the piece, and a couple of proposals and project descriptions had been written for funding applications, which established a territory of exploration. Hannah had also done a try-out of some related ideas at HATCH in Leicester, which I had seen, so we had an idea of how we would use a computer (screen).

At the start of our two weeks at Northern Stage in February, I set Hannah a warm up exercise. We set the space up with our regular tools: a table, couple of chairs, laptop, projector and screen. We had asked almost arbitrarily for a couple of lighting states (and then Kev and the team at Northern Stage had made Stage 2 look beautiful).

On the table I laid out a series of 24 prompts or questions, written on index cards, face down. These prompts were all born out of our discussions so far, so Hannah was clearly 'able' to answer them, but she was to respond in the moment as she turned each card. This is a mode of being 'put on the spot' but within a territory you are informed about and comfortable in, that we have used in the making of a number of Third Angel projects. I find it can help performers not worry about whether or not what they're doing is "any good", and just get some material and ideas out into the process.

I thought this would fill a couple of hours on the afternoon of the first day, and give us something to talk about on day 2. It took a week. A performed live research process that discovered the rules of the space, of the piece. Hannah instinctively started using the internet live, explaining what she was doing, sometimes, just quickly sourcing a reference at others.

On one level the show is formally similar to *A Conversation With…*: there's a screen, a projector, some video material, a table and a couple of chairs and Hannah tells a story. But the way these ingredients are used feels quite distinct, to me. Hannah's relationship to the screen, to us, is different.

The text.

This piece is the first one in which I almost completely improvise. There's no text which I riff off, rather there lay on the floor in front of me a series of index cards, each marking a chapter in the story. As the show progresses, I move along the cards, telling each story (not wildly differently – you fall into a pattern, you edit yourself, learning what works and what doesn't, what's necessary for pacing and understanding). For that reason there is no script, instead, what I have here, is a transcript of the final work in progress showing from autumn 2015. It's totally verbatim, with a description of my actions in italics when it's not clear from the text. It's therefore full of the ungainly repetitions and the ums and ahs and 'so's of everyday speech. I offer it un-amended in that respect. However, as I begin and end the show saying: this is not just my story. This is the story of all the people I meet on the journey. It felt right, therefore, that I offer room for the people involved to comment on how they were a part of my story. So after the transcript, you can read the following extra bits of writing:

- An exchange of emails between Angela Hibbs and me.
- A thought from David Lamb, brother of John.

- A conversation with my brother, Lawrence Nicklin, about the day of the Outlaw
- A conversation with my Mother, Linda Nicklin, about the day of the Outlaw.
- An excerpt from my interview with Phil Hayes, sports scientist at Northumbria University
- An excerpt from my interview with Sarah Partington sports psychologist at Northumbria University.
- An excerpt from a blog post (soon to be a book) by Emily Chappell, about her experience of the Transcontinental bike race. "Transcontinental: Night on Bald Mountain".

This is dedicated to all those people, but most of all, this story is told in the memory of John Lamb.

HANNAH NICKLIN

Equations for a Moving Body

Transcript, October 2015, Carriageworks.

The Audience enter. Hannah is sat at a laptop, the screen is shared, projected behind her. The music that people enter to is a mix from Hannah's Bandcamp account. She is picking songs, reading lyrics, opening tabs, deciding what to play next, selecting a new track just as the previous one ends.

The show starts. She fades down the music with her volume button. She says hello to the audience. Welcomes them to Equations for a Moving Body.

When she begins, she closes all the tabs from Bandcamp. But from there on in, every site or page she brings up will be in a new tab, the old tabs left up.

This is for Sarah. For John. For T-Cass. For Angela, for Phil, for Simon. For Emily. For Chris and Elliott. Lawrence, who is my brother, and my mum.

So it's 2.30 P.M. on the 10th of February 2015, and I'm on the second floor of the Life Sciences building at the University of Northumbria. I'm there to meet Dr Sarah Partington. She's a sports psychologist; she's keen to emphasise this. I call her a sports scientist at the beginning of the conversation and she says, "No, actually I'm a sports psychologist." I do believe that psychology is a science, but in the spirit of self-identification obviously, we're going to call her a sports psychologist. It's a specialism.

One of the first things I do is that I show Sarah a video.

This video.

Hannah Googles Sian Welch and Wendy Ingram and the autocomplete suggests the video. The video shows 2 women less than 1km from the finish line of an Ironman, repeatedly falling,

122

and struggling to get up, and then eventually, crawling to the finish line.

So this is the 1997 Ironman World Championship. We're currently watching Wendy Ingram. Wendy Ingram is in the final part of her race. Before this point she has swum 2.4 miles, cycled 112, and she's in the final part of her marathon.

Wendy is currently in fourth place.

She's only a couple of hundred metres form the finish line, and in a second, she's going to spot... Sian Welch. There. The woman in fifth.

That's the finish mat. 15 metres.

And there. That's the decision that wins Sian fourth place.

5th.

I show Sarah this video, and I ask her: "What makes us do that? What makes us put ourselves through that, take ourselves to that point, to the point where you collapse and you get up. And you collapse, and you get up. And you collapse, and you cannot get up again, and so you crawl?" And Sarah, she talks to me about a theory called The Storied Self. She said it's a theory among others, but it's one that she specialises in. She says that we are storytelling animals, that the way we construct our identities is looking at everything that has happened to us in our lives, and choosing what's important. What's key to our story? What's important to us about the things that have happened to us, and ratifying our identity by telling our stories to others. We get to practise our idea of who we are through storytelling.

Sarah says that when you take a goal on into your life, when you build it into every day, through training or the things you choose to eat and when you go to bed and the people that you spend time with, when you take a goal on into your life, you make that goal part of your story, part of who you are. If you don't reach that goal, she says, and she uses these exact words; "It can shatter your identity." Shatter.

She talks about working with athletes, pro athletes, who expect a certain trajectory out of their careers, so they go to juniors, to seniors, and then they compete as an elite athlete, and they expect a certain trajectory there as well, that you will get better and better, and you will be selected for the right squads, and then there will be a peak, and then you decline, but maybe then you retrain as a coach and help other people become better.

She says that the people that don't reach that bit, the pinnacle, the top, the expected place where you stop, people whose careers are interrupted by serious injuries, she says it can shatter their identities – you have to do a lot of work rebuilding their sense of self. She also talks about the difference between extrinsic and intrinsic motivation, so extrinsic motivations are things outside of us, things like a prize, like a car or some money. Intrinsic motivation, that stuff that reinforces our sense of self.

Sport, she says, is largely an intrinsically rewarding activity, because as you're doing it, it's confirming that goal that you've taken on as part of yourself. She says there's a state called 'flow'. Flow is how you describe undergoing intrinsically rewarding activity; a state of flow is also used in game design theory to describe that feeling you get where you're just getting a little bit better; you're beating it, just about, by a hair's breadth, you're holding on. That feeling of excitement, that rush – you get that in sport too.

In that state of intrinsically rewarding activity, in that state of flow, your sense of environment and health can vanish – it's just you, and that goal which is the story of you.

Another thing Sarah says to me in that way, when you realise that a psychologist has been listening, like regular people don't do, she says to me: "You've said a couple of times that you're a swimmer. That seems important to you." I am a swimmer. I have always swum. I grew up swimming, from the age if 3 or 4, before I could even remember, I was a member of City of Lincoln Pentaqua, which was a swimming club in my home town

Hannah Googles 'Pentaqua', brings up the club website.

– I was a member of it with my brother. I wore this exact logo – they have not changed it in the 25 years since I started swimming for them – on a black silicone hat, every morning and every evening for a good portion of my life.

Swimming is a small kind of superpower. Me and my little brother, we realised this when we went to Center Parcs for the first time. For the first time we were surrounded by people who weren't members of our club in the swimming pool. They struggled; they were scared about breathing, they would hold their head up and therefore sink. They didn't understand about buoyancy; we would move through the water like we were moving through air, it was no different to us. That holiday, we discovered we had a small kind of superpower.

I'm a swimmer, but part of my story is also how I had to give it up. I was 12-years-old at the time and we were going on our first abroad holiday in a caravan. We were going to France. We were staying over in Poole on a campsite before going over on a ferry the next day. There was a climbing frame there as part of the playground. I climbed it, I fell off, I put my arms out to stop my head hitting the ground. They did their job, and in doing so they buckled.

2 breaks, in both bones, in both arms. There's a picture, I think, in my old photos on Facebook of me with 2 broken arms.

Hannah goes onto Facebook, and finds the album 'old photos' via her profile as she talks.

We didn't make it abroad that year. We stayed on the campsite though, mostly in order to be near the hospital. My dad squeezed into my bunk bed as I slept in the double bed with my mum so I had room. She said she would wake up to find the sheets tangled around my feet, that I had been swimming in my sleep.

We went back to Lincoln, and 4 weeks in, I had an x-ray and the discovered that the arms, they weren't setting properly – so they had to re-break them. The re-broke my arms, and pinned them, and I was in a cast for another 6 weeks. By the time I got into the pool, I think three months had passed. It felt good to be home for a little while, but I was so out of training I had to move down several sets – and, if I'm honest, swimming hurt.

My mum used to take me to training, She was there in every bit of my journey through sport, driving me to places early in the morning. She says to me that she has a really strong memory of watching me, just after I got back into training, at Yarborough Pool, trying to get out of the water. My whole life, getting out of a pool was as simple as swimming up to the edge, putting my hands down, pushing up and over – never in my life would it occur to me to use the steps. My mum watched me swim up to the side and put my hands on the edge.

I just didn't have the strength.

So I'm 28-years-old when I said out loud for the first time: "I am going to do an Ironman." I don't know at this point that Ironman is the brand, not the distance, but that's what I say out loud. I say it to a friend of a friend who I am trying to learn some stuff about cycling from.

Hannah goes over to the laptop and creates a grid into which she enters the different distances

If you don't know, if you've not heard of triathlon, or maybe you've heard of it but you don't know exactly what it involves, it's one single event in which you begin by swimming, and then you cycle, and then you run. So there are different distances of triathlon, and at the age of 28 when I say it out loud for the first time, "I am going to do a Ironman," I had done a sprint triathlon, which involves – well, my one did at least – in Lincolnshire, I did a 400m pool swim, followed by a 24km bike ride, followed by a 5k run.

I was training for, at that point, when I said out loud for the first time, "I am going to do an Ironman," I was training for the lead standard, or Olympic distance. That would be the distance that you see like the Brownlee brothers do in the Commonwealth and the Olympics. That involves… it's now an open water swim, the lead standard in particular, there is a little variation in distances, but they're around this: 1,500 metres of swimming in open water, followed by a 42km ride, followed by a 9km or 10km run.

Then there is the middle distance – it sort of switches over to miles now, I don't know if they tried to make the distances sound less threatening by putting them into miles, so I'm going to try and give you both, but forgive me if my translation isn't quite like, down pat. So it's a 1.2-mile swim, which must be around 1,800 metres, followed by a – because 1,500 metres is a mile in a pool, but that's actually different to regular miles, so… don't ask me why – then a 56-mile cycle ride, and a half marathon, a half marathon being… it's 21km… I'm just going to leave half marathon up there, and you'll have to forgive me on the maths. So 56 miles. When I did the Cotswold Middle Distance, that was actually an 84, that's not a direct translation of 56 miles, I know that, so that's a 21km ride, er, run.

So the final one is the Iron Distance, but you Iron because it's a brand, so it's actually a full distance, or sometimes called a long-distance triathlon. So that's what I meant when I said Ironman. That's a 2.4-mile swim, followed by a 112-mile cycle, followed by a – ha-ha, I'm getting into kilometres straight away – so the marathon, the full marathon, which is 26.2 miles. So that works out at roughly – it really is rough – 3,800 metres, 184 is what my Garmin had recorded, and 42 kilometres of running.

I'm 28-years-old when I say out loud for the first time: "I am going to do an Ironman." And the second that I say it, something clicks. Because I've been thinking about it for a while, not quite knowing why I want to do this, and in saying it out loud, I don't just say, "I am going to do an Ironman," I say, "In the year that I turn 30, I am going to do an Ironman." And it's right there.

We're surrounded by all these stories of who we should be, the things we should do by what age, the things we should own... I'm pretty reconciled with the fact that I'm never going to be able to own a house. I can't even drive, for one thing! I'm not interested in getting married, I'm not sure if I want children, I don't think you could describe what I do as a career. And I'm okay with stepping back from the milestones that we were told our lives should be, but that doesn't mean I don't want any of my own. It doesn't mean I don't want chapter headings.

So I'm 28-years-old when I say out loud for the first time, "I am going to do an Ironman," and I realise in that moment that what I want is a milestone of my own, for being 30 with.

A year later, at the age of 29, I sign up to the Outlaw. A full-distance triathlon which will occur on the 26th of July, 2015.

So I'm a swimmer. I've always swum. But obviously I also cycle, and I run. Running is the thing that I came to second.

Running is something that was gifted to me by my friend John. John is a friend I met in the early days of Twitter. 5 or 6 years ago, Twitter was a different place – it as friendlier, smaller, you could come across people more easily, and not just based on your proximity, suddenly I was able to make friends according to my interests or the cadences of our sense of humour. I've got some good friends now, best friends who were people I met in the early days of Twitter. John is one of the people I met in the early days of Twitter.

A few years after meeting him, getting to know him, maybe 4 years later, I'm at Loughborough University studying for a PhD. I've started swimming again, primarily because the swimming pool at Loughborough University is absolutely irresistible.

As she talks, Hannah goes to the computer, and Googles 'Loughborough University Pool' it autocompletes and she clicks 'images', selects an image to fill the screen

It's this beautiful 50m pool, because they are technically the home of British swimming, it's brand new, it's huge... it feels good.

So I'm enjoying getting used to swimming again and finding muscle memories that I didn't know that I had, and I'm taking sneaky peeks at all of British Swimming people training, and trying to just copy bits of their technique. And then after a while, I've got this energy, and sometimes the pool is closed or there aren't any lanes, so I decide that I'll go for a run. Everyone in Loughborough seems to be running everywhere anyway, so why not give it a go? Not with any sense of doing it though, it's something I do because I can't do something else – it's not a thing that's mine.

Hannah goes over and Googles 'Fitocracy' – she brings up the site, she's logged on already, it looks quite inactive.

Around the time that I was studying my PhD, I joined something called Fitocracy. Now, Fitocracy is essentially a means of gamifying sport – it's points for sport. It's a social network, and what you do is you upload details of your workouts, so you might tell it you've gone for a run, you tell it how far you went, how fast you went when you did it, so how long it took you, you might tell it the terrain, other variables, and it will use that information and some algorithms to generate you some points for it. Obviously points are rad, but points aren't really fun unless you've got people to beat them with, so what I did was I invited a bunch of my friends to join me, like half of them ignored me, which is totally fine, and they were like... a quarter joined but never did anything, which is like an extra nice way of going, "I don't care but I like you," and then a couple of people did join in.

My friend V from Manchester, and John from Edinburgh, we struck up a friendly rivalry. Because every time I put a swim in it would be this amazing amount of points, and every time I put a run in it would be this little, piddly like 100 or 200, and John was a runner who was learning to swim, so he would do amazing runs across the hills of Edinburgh and surrounding areas, and every time he put a swimming lesson in it would get him like 50 or 100 points at best. We were well-matched.

We rose up through the ranks; there was a point at which I was the 14th highest-scoring woman in the world on Fitocracy – that's how bad it got. Eventually we got a bit tired of it, but the thing that it revealed to us was that I'm a swimmer who was trying to get better at running, and he was a runner who was trying to get better at swimming, so we thought, "Why not do a training weekend?" Why not hang out together and share skills? So that's what we did.

It was November. I remember that it was November because, in the evening of the Saturday, I put on a Bing Crosby

Christmas record, and he groaned at me. So it was too early for Christmas records, but late enough that I wanted to put one on, so I'm going to go with late November.

Back to the image of the pool

The first thing we did was that we went swimming in my beautiful pool. There are four lanes at Loughborough, but contrary to everywhere else, they don't call them slow, middle, middle, fast, they call them slow, medium, fast and very fast, which is their thing. It made him laugh. I got into the very fast lane and I did a quick 3k as he got used to the pool, then I hopped into his lane and had a look at his technique. Now, John is a very long man, a long, tall, thin man, very good body for running with, but you put those people in water they usually they just sink. They sort of sag in the middle, and then by the time you're doing this, you're like, "I'm not going to be able to breathe," and then your head goes up, and as soon as your head goes up you're just more likely to sink.

Swimming is about equilibrium; it's about balance. In a world of thickened fluid dynamics, swimming is about holding your central line, it's about body position, high in the water. The second you sag, you sink. The second you bring your head up because you're scared you might not be able to breathe, you change your body position into something flat. It's useful to think about the way that birds fly in air; that's how you need to move through water. There's a reason birds don't fly like this.

So I gave him some drills. Drills that will just help him understand what his body should feel like when it was at the right position. So that's using floats. So you might do some kick with a kick board in front of you, but instead of having your head up while you do it, you head down kick and you hold it in front of you like that, and that means that you're head is at the right position it should be while most of the stroke is happening.

There's lots of things you can do with kick to strengthen your kick, because the kick will be the thing that stops you dragging with your feet. So a good kick will set you right again. Holding on to the edge of the wall and just kicking, and feeling how your body raises and falls, that's a good way to get used to that.

And then breathing drills, because breathing is just as important as body position because breathing is the thing that can disrupt your body position. So, one-arm drills, when you hold a float out in front of you, you kick, and your job is just to breathe.

We went through some drills, then went home to listen to some Bing Crosby. The next day was the running day. I picked a route that was 21km, because I'd done it once before, it was the furthest that I'd run ever, I thought like I would just try and, you know, quietly impress John with the distances that I could do, so I picked a route I knew that was a half marathon.

At the time, I lived at 8, Hastings Street.

She types in the address and brings up Google Maps, she selects the Google Earth view for a moment

Number 8 with the blue door, 8 being my favourite number and blue being my favourite colour, I always liked that house.

She returns to map view, and as she describes the route they took, follows it on the map. Dragging it along the path they run.

So... it was a heavy grey day and we came out of my house, turned left onto Oxford Road, then right onto Station Street. Then onto the Derby Road but not for long; you turn right at Domino's onto Belton Road, and just here there's a little set of steps that take you down to beside the canal. You run alongside the canal for a while, then just here there's a bridge, a rickety bridge, that takes you down to a dirt path – you've been previously running on tarmac. That dirt path is really muddy; Leicestershire is flat and it floods a lot down here by the canal and the river. Fitocracy at the time didn't have a variable for mud, but it does make it quite hard, so I've been putting my runs in as 'slightly hilly' even though they were blatantly not, and John in Edinburgh had been teasing me about this, but as soon as we got to the mud he went, "All right – I'll give you that."

So we followed the canal round, eventually it joins the River Soar and becomes the river proper.

Follow the river a little more, past Normanton-on-Soar, and then here there's a weir which I always like because it made the air smell of water. You cross over one little road, then it joins a canal which is not really a canal, it's technically the river, but there's loads of canal boats moored there and a lock at the end. A style here, which you cross over, and then there's a big field which is full of these scary-looking cows that just stare at you as you go by.

You follow the river up, and eventually it curves to the right – that's where the anglers sit in the summer. A little bit further, you run through the back of a stately home, and then there's a weir and a lock, and if you turn around at that point, that's 21 km out and back.

We run.

Hannah gets back up

We run through the fields and mud of Leicestershire. He's a lot faster than me, and it's easier to be faster than someone in a pool because your laps are only 25 or 50 metres. So what he did was, he would pick a point in the distance, run up to it, and run back to me, over and over again. After he'd got rid of some energy, he then started taking me through technique. He watched me as I ran for a little while, and then he gave me really helpful suggestions for how to correct my technique. I had been reading stuff online, but not nearly clicking with me.

He said things like, "Watch your shadow in the sun." The sun was low, and he said, "Look at the shadow that you cast. When you run, if your shadow's bobbing up and down a lot, you are putting energy into going up and not across – so just try and watch your shadow and keep it low, and send your energy forwards rather than up." He looked at my cadence, and gave me recommendations, drills I could do to improve my cadence, talked about intervals, made me run from intervals as we went.

We turned around, and started running back. Past the scary-looking cows, and then at the weir, just before Normanton-on-Soar, John raised his pace. I was already running quite fast, if I'm honest, in the way that you do when you're running with someone new and trying to impress. He raises his pace. There are around 5km to go, and I go, "Maybe he's not noticed," so I try and match it, just about I can manage. Then 4km to go, just past Normanton-on-Soar, and he raises it again, and I go, "Okay, this is on purpose. Well, in that case, I'll match it." That's a different reaction that I have.

Then there are 3km to go – I don't know how he's judging the distances so perfectly, I'm the one with the watch that says how far we'd gone. 3km to go, just as the canal splits off from the river, and he raises his pace again, and I think, "This is the limit of it – this is all that I can hold." 2km to go, and again. 1km, just after we got past from the dirt path onto tarmac, he raises the pace again. We get to the steps and there are 800m to go, and I'm glad for the rest. "I'm just going to go slowly up them because I think I might trip."

And then we're running again, and there are 600m to go, and the Belton Road and the blue of Domino's, and he raises the pace again and we're basically sprinting. We cross the Derby Road, for the first time in my life there's no traffic to stop us, and I curse it. There are 600, 500, 400 metres to go. Oxford Street. There are 400, 300, 200 metres to go and we're at Station Street. There is 100, 100 metres to go, and I can see Hastings Street. 50. 25. My blue door. 10. I feel like my eyeballs are bleeding. 5.

We hit the door, and I try and catch my breath. I fumble for my keys in my pocket, and we fall in.

Just before we set out, I'd put some bread going in the bread maker. We have hot bread with melted butter and pints of orange squash. Covered in the mud of Leicestershire.

It just feels really… honest.

So, cycling is the thing that I came to last. I've always been a swimmer, and running is something that my friend John gave me. Cycling is something that I had to take for myself.

So 3 years ago, I moved to London. At that time, I'm training for the Leeds standard – 42km of riding, longest that I'll have ridden at that point – and I'm complaining to a friend that I don't know how to train on London roads, it's full of traffic lights, and taxi drivers and buses just seem to want to see me die. How am I supposed to get any pace? And he says, "You should go out with Tom." T-Cass, Tom Cassidy, T-Cass for short. "He goes out all the time, into Kent and Surrey. He'll take you out."

So that's what brings me to just outside Greenwich Foot Tunnel. I'm there on my aluminium, black Trek bike with the pink bar tape, and T-Cass rolls up on his white B'twin, wearing a King of the Mountains jersey. If you don't know, follow the Tour de France, the King of the Mountains jersey is white with red polka dots, and it's for the person who wins the most hill stages; it's for the climber.

Tom is a climber. He takes me out, and the first hill that we hit is Shooter's Hill. There are hills in London, it turns out. It's hard. I struggle up it and spend the next half hour going, "Huh! That hill!" until we get to the North Kent Downs.

There are the set of four hills in one go, all categorised – they're category 4 – and they go from one to the other to the next… there's just no easy way to do them. He takes me up this set of four hills. I'm scared. I'm a girl from Lincolnshire, I am scared of hills in any case. I struggle. It gets hard; I keep on trying to change down a gear but there are no more left. I feel like… I sound like I'm having a fatal asthma attack, and Tom, he seems like he's governed by this different kind of gravity, he just sort of slinks up, and then notices that I've dropped back and then falls back again. He looks at me for a moment. He says, "You're a swimmer, aren't you?" I mean to say the word 'yes' but some kind of unidentifiable noise comes out. He goes, "You've got strong arms, then. Use them. Climbing is as much about your arms as is it about your legs – get out of the saddle, pull your shoulders back, and use your arms. Pull."

I do what he says. It's hard, but I feel in control of the difficulty of it. There's something about the care of sharing training with others, the care you take of one another, of injuries, of people who are less experienced than you. There's something there that I really enjoy.

So it's 6 months later, and it's one month since Tom and I broke up. I'm getting up early because I have to go to a meeting later that day in Sheffield. I want to get a ride in – I'm trying to ride because I don't want cycling to be the thing that a boy gave me, I want it to be my thing. I want it to be mine. So I'm going out for a ride. I get out of bed, and my eyes are thick with hay fever and pollution – it's early spring. I put my dressing gown on and then I just kneel down on the rug by my bed, and then I just put my arms on the rug, and then my head, and I get another 10 minutes' sleep before my second alarm goes off on the rug next to my bed.

Training is hard. I train every day apart from one rest day a week, and it's hard to go out every day. The only reason I go out every day is because I'm someone who goes out every day. The day that I don't will be the day that I stop. So I'm late. I wolf down a breakfast and I pull my bike gear on. I head out. Turn right out of Hither Green into Lewisham, then down to Deptford. Turn left into Peckham. It's rush hour, there's lots of angry, silly traffic on the streets. For example, in Peckham, there's this long, straight road, long like of stationary traffic that's just sort of creeping along occasionally, and a nice, lovely, clear bike lane all the way. There's a brief gap in the traffic because there's a road that comes off the main road, and some… one woman decides that she's going to try and cut through it real quickly, because she thinks that this creeping car is going to stop her for like two seconds, so she shoots through it just as I am coming up on my bike. We both brake hard, and my front wheel hits her bonnet. It's not bent or anything, we've both braked in time, but I give her two thumps, and a look that said, "We both know you nearly just killed me," before I ride on. By the time I get to Vauxhall Bridge I'm shaking. By the time I cross the river again at Battersea it's sort of worn off. I ride up to Richmond.

Richmond Park is beautiful; there are deer in it. It's a 10k loop. It's a good place to go if you're a bit late because you can always cut a lap off if you're running out of time. Depending on the different times of day you go to Richmond, you ride with different people. So at the weekend, it's the Weekend Warriors – it's the city boys with five grand bikes, or the fathers getting some resistance training in with a trailer of their kids on the back. If you go in the week, it's the old boys. Old boys in old team kits, their steel bicycles, they waltz up the climbs. Just the old boys and the freelancers. I ride with them.

I cut off one lap, so I only do 30k in the park before my now 25km back. I find my exit. I head out. A flash of red and white. I know it's not him. I know it's not him. It's not his bike. I ride on. Just as the road from Richmond meets Lordship Lane, the bit where Lordship Lane meets the Horniman Museum and heads down into Forest Hill again – now that is a hill. It's not the hardest hill in the city, but it's a tough one – people know it. And I know that it's a segment on Strava.

In case you don't know, Strava...

Hannah goes over to the laptop, and throughout the next, takes the audience through Strava, a particular activity on her account, segments, etc.

I guess is a bit of a Fitocracy successor for me, this is the place that I now record all of the sport that I do. Strava is... it takes the GPS on a phone, but it can use like a bike computer or a wrist computer, but you can just use a phone. It takes the GPS and records where you go, and then using time, it can tell how fast you went where you went. As soon as you complete an activity, you hit 'Go' and then you hit 'Finish' and Strava uploads to the site.

So let's have a look at one of my recent rides. Actually, let's... because that was just a run, which is not as fun. Okay. So this is a ride that I did last month. As soon as something's uploaded, it's split up into segments. Anyone can put a segment into Strava, all you have to do is say where it starts, where it finishes, and click 'Go' and anyone who has ever been through that segment will be measured against it.

So let's find a reasonably well-worn... okay, so this is one of the official 100 climbs in the UK according to some book. It's actually called Kidd's Hill, but sometimes it's called 'The Wall', and this is a segment on Strava. So there are 6,949 people who've gone through it. I am 3,724th, although if you put me in the field of just women I'm doing a little bit better. You can add in a bunch of things, so you can use a heart rate monitor or you can put power and cadence measures on your bike – it's incredibly nerdy, but hopefully you understand what a segment is – it's a little bit of space which people are measured through on Strava when they use it when they're riding a bike. So I'm coming up to where Lordship Lane turns into the Horniman Museum, and down into Forest Hill again, and I know that this is a segment on Strava. I also know… I also know that Tom is top 10 on it. I think, "Fuck it." For the first time in my life I don't change down – I change up. I don't sit, scared that I won't have the energy to get to the top, I lay it all out on the road. I ride hard. I get out of the saddle – that familiar, eyeballs bleeding feeling that you get when you are at max effort. I hit the summit, and for the first time in my life I've earned the descent. The wind cools me as I roll down into Forest Hill, back through Catford, into Hither Green, and I plug my Garmin into my computer. Strava says I've equalled it. I've equalled his time. I think, "Fine, that's not beating it but that'll do."

I head to my meeting. On the train to Sheffield, I look at the landscape through the window and I think, "That looks like it would be fun to ride." My right leg starts to tighten a little, so I surreptitiously try and stretch it under the seats. I get to my meeting, I go, I get on the train back. My leg is really stiffening now. By the time I'm at King's Cross I have to limp my way across the night buses back to Lewisham. The next day I can't move it. I go to a physio and he says I have a 'category 4 tear'. Um. I don't tell him how I did it. I don't tell him that it was worth it.

Tom, he showed me the hills of Kent and Surrey, but it was up to me to take them.

Angela is a runner. Angela is contemplating her last run. It's 9.30 A.M. on the 6th of February 2015 and I'm in a café on the University of Northumbria campus, just across from the swimming pool that I swam in earlier that morning. I'm meeting Dr Angela Hibbs, who's a brilliant, brilliant sports scientist who has put me in contact with a bunch of other sports scientists and psychologists for my project.

Angela specialises in bio-mechanics. She talks about the different kinetic chains involved when you cycle, swim and run; cycling is a fixed kinetic chain, and swimming and running are open ones. She tells me about the different things that affect performance, so nutrition is much more key than people think. Then there's training, and then there's genetics.

Angela knows that it's her genes that are the problem, because her sister, who's never run a day in her life, has bad knees too. In Angela's left knee there is almost no cartilage remaining. She was on track for a 2:45 in the Berlin marathon, but she says she's got one last run left in her.

She says she doesn't want to 'break' herself, she says she wants to be able to run after her kids when they're little, if she has some, so she says she's allowing herself one more long run. She's saving it for Ironman Bolton. So I'm signed up to the Outlaw. On the 26th of July 2015, I will attempt the Outlaw triathlon. 7 days before that, the Sunday before, Angela will attempt Ironman Bolton. I ask her why. Why is she saving her last long run for this? And she says, "Well, number 1, it's every endurance athlete's pinnacle, isn't it?" The full distance triathlon. The Ironman. She says, "Two, because I've got... I know people who have done it, people who are less fit than I am, who are less good; if they can do it, why can't I?" And she says, "Because I want to know what it feels like, crossing that red carpet."

2 days after Ironman Bolton I get an email. There are 5 days until my competition. She did it. She did it in a frankly astonishing time of 12 hours and 15. She was top 3 of her age group, so she stayed behind in order to be at the awards ceremony. She said her quads are never going to forgive her, and she gives me advice. Advice like I should drink flat coke towards the end of the race, that your body just can't deal with solids, so if you find flat coke on the feed stations, just keep on drinking it. She says the last 10 miles are just hard, but you get through it.

Angela is a runner.

Angela used her last run in Ironman Bolton.

**Break from 59:32 to 65:32 where 'Falling' happens –
a silent section of just live Googling:**

Hannah sits down.
She googles 'John Lamb, Chamonix'
She picks a headline. It's purple, the link has been clicked before.
"Tributes paid to snowboarder who fell to his death in France"
There is a picture of John
Scroll.
"FAMILY and friends have paid tribute to a Scots snowboarder
who died after falling from an isolated ridge in the French Alps.
John Lamb plummeted 3600ft after getting into difficulties on a
path close to the summit of Mont Blanc as he returned from the
last run of his five-month holiday in Chamonix."
The article continues.
Back
Hannah type twitter.com/lawnjam
The most recent tweet is the 22nd of April 2013
Scroll
Scroll
Hannah clicks on an Instagram link
She clicks on his profile
Scroll
She fullscreens a selfie with ice in his beard from a cold run in
the snow.
She goes back to the tab with the article
She highlights '3600ft'
New tab. Google: 'equations for a falling body'
Finds a Wikipedia article
Finds the equation for calculating the time it takes to fall a
distance 'd'
Copies
Open a notepad tab
Pastes in the equation
Returns to the article, finds a value for gravity, inserts it in the
equation

Finds the distance fallen, pastes it in.
Googles '3600ft in m'
Copies the distance in m, inserts in the equation
She completes the equation using the google calculator function.
She has a value for 't'.
She goes back to the tab of the photo of him
She googles 'timer'
Google timer
She sets the timer to 't'
She watches.
An alarm goes off.
She stops it.
She sets the timer to 't'
She watches.
An alarm goes off.
Longer this time.
She stops.
New tab.

Hannah goes on flickr, image gallery 'Outlaw 2015', brings up the first photo, of a sunrise over the lake

It's 4.30. 4.30A.M. on the 26th July, 2015, and I am early. Too early. Me, my mum, my brother, in my mum's car, are the first of like five cars on-site. The sun is just rising. The day of the Outlaw. I've set my bike and all of my gear up in relative bags in transition the day before, but nevertheless I go down and I check them 3, 4, 5, 6 times each.

There's still an hour to go though, before I really need to be getting into my wetsuit. It's summer, but cold, because it's early. I stand, my mum and my brother stand either side of me, hugging me to keep me warm. After a while, time passes. It's time to go down. I go back to transition, I check all of my bags again, 2, 3, 4 times, and then that's it. I put my wetsuit on. I hand my day clothes over to a marshal and I go over to the side of the lake.

People are gathering there. There are 1,449 others awkwardly adjusting their wetsuits. I have got my goggles and two hats in my hands. I put one red silicone hat on top of my head and then I put my goggles over the top of that, and on top of those, in order to keep the goggles in place, because you don't want to lose them when you're in a lake, I put the official Outlaw swim hat. It's silver, silicone, and it says on the side, in orange – just in case you've forgotten – the distances. 2.4 miles. 112. 26.2. We're by a lake, which is just to one side from bike transition where all the bikes are racked, and then there's the boat house, on which I can see my mum and my brother, and I'm really glad to see them again one more time before I get in the water. I spend some time trying to attract their attention, even recruiting people around me, because they just can't see me. And then my brother finally spots me, which is why we have this photo.

Next photo

At about ten to six, the crowd of people begins to move slowly forwards. We move to the front of the lake where there are one of four bays. You get into a bay according to the time you expect to swim. So the first bay, bay number one, is for people who expect to swim a sub one hour 2.4 miles. I get into the second one, which is for people who expect to swim between one hour and 1 hour 15. I'm expecting maybe a 1.07, or even a 1.10 if there are lots of people in my way. A personal best would be 1.05.

Next photo

We get in the water. Then there are 5 minutes of treading water awkwardly with strangers. I spend time checking with the people around me, just find out what kind of times they're expecting, so I'm in the right kind of area of the bay, so I'm not going to get into anyone's way. There's someone on the side, on the bank. He's got a klaxon and looks official.

He's getting the crowd to cheer us, and then he gets us to wave in one direction and wave in the other.

I've been thinking about this moment for two years. I've been training for it for nine months. I have been in mortal terror of it for at least five weeks.

But right now I'm not scared.

I'm a swimmer in water.

The klaxon goes. My job now is to swim.

So five weeks, five months rather, before this point, on the 6th of February 2015, at 1.30P.M., I meet Dr Phil Hayes in his office on the second floor of the Northumbria University Life Sciences Building. And he eats his lunch.

He apologises that he needs to have a sandwich while we talk; it's lunch break. This is the only moment he's had for me. He's really eager to talk to me though. I ask him lots of questions about endurance sport, that's what he specialises in, including particularly endurance running, but he also works with triathletes. I ask him, amongst other things, what happens to our bodies when we train? One of the first things he says is that rest and recovery is as important in training, to training, to the things that you actually do when you train.

He says a lot of people don't rest enough.

And then he talks about the changes, the actual physical changes that you make to your body when you train. The first thing he says is that we grow our hearts. The heart is a muscle, and when we train, we increase our cardiovascular capacity. How much blood is moved around our body with each stroke – that's important because our muscles, the ones we recruit when we do the sport, they need blood, because they need oxygen, that's how we deliver it round our body. They need oxygen because the muscles, the cells in the muscles, they make energy out of oxygen plus either fats or carbohydrates – glycogen. It takes either fats or carbohydrates and puts them together with oxygen to produce energy and carbon dioxide, which is taken away to be breathed out.

So when we recruit muscles, they demand oxygen. So we increase our cardiovascular capacity, more blood moves with each stroke, and we also increase the number and the size of the capillaries around the muscles, so a greater surface area the oxygen can transfer over. And then finally, we change the actual insides, the structures of the cells themselves, so we get more muscle cells, but there are changes in them.

Apologies for anyone who has like, gone beyond GCSE biology. I'm just going to really check in with everyone and not assume that everyone knows what a cell looks like.

Hannah draws it on the screen using a tablet and drawing program online

So like, basically, a cell's a bit rounder than that basically, but that's a cell. And the edge is called a membrane. In the heart of it there's this thing that you call a nucleus, that's where all the genetic information and instructions are stored, and then in the middle there's kind of a goo thing which I remember being called cytoplasm – I don't know if it's pronounced like that, that's just how I read it in my biology book. In that, there are intramuscular – so this is a muscle cell – there are intramuscular stores of fats and carbohydrates that are actually stored as glycogen and as fat in the cell themselves. So part of training builds those intramuscular stores up. You also store it in your liver, and fats themselves are stored in adipose tissue, fat tissue.

Phil says that when you train, the bit of your cell that is the thing that makes the energy grows. They're called mitochondria, and they are the things that take the oxygen and hopefully the glycogen, because fat is harder to process, but it takes those things together and makes energy. When you train, you increase the size and the number of the mitochondria.

When Phil told me this I was like, "Cool, okay, that sounds interesting." And then he was like, "You've not followed, have you?" and I said, "Sort of." He said, "Think of the cell as like a sink. The limiting factor is not the amount of oxygen you can deliver to it. So think of turning on a tap as much as you like. You can keep on turning it, and the sink will fill up. The mitochondria are like plugholes. If there are only a few plugholes and they're quite small, that sink will fill up quite fast, overflow, and then the extra oxygen will be taken away to be exhaled. If you increase the size and the number of plugholes, way more energy can be produced. Greater throughput."

Then I got it. That made sense.

And it was all super interesting, but the thing that really stuck with me, the thing that I hadn't thought of in that way before, was that the heart is a muscle.

Back to the photos of the Outlaw

It's a couple of minutes past six on the 26th of July 2015, and my job now is to swim. I've been really nervous because I haven't started with as many people before; I've usually gone out in waves at swim starts, so maybe there are 250 people, that's the maximum that I've swum with. This is everyone starting at the same time. 1,450 people in the water. I've been worrying about getting a broken nose, I've been worrying about getting knocked out and drowning and no-one noticing, I've been worrying about getting a black eye. But actually, when it starts, it's fine.

So for a little while, I do what we call water polo stroke, so a head up front crawl so I can sort of see where I'm going and notice where people are, who might swim into me. For a while that gets me sort of round the edge of the bay, the group that I started with, and then suddenly I'm sort of at the front of it. One guy – now, I don't like him – one guy decides to get hold of my shoulder and dunk me. He actually dunks me, there's really no need for that. He pushes me under the water and swims over. That's the worst it gets, and it's fine because quite quickly I catch him up and take him over again. I'm on the edge. I'm at the front of the second bay of people, and suddenly they drop away – they're not really with me any more; it's just me and the water doing something I know how to do, something I do, something I do… the water is cool and clear, the sun has risen, and it's warm, and the water is just the right temperature. For the first time in a long time, I'm breathing comfortably, bilaterally, three to one, so that's one, two, three, breathe, one, two, three… it's a better way to breathe because it balances out your stroke, but I've struggled, always, to swim in open water bilaterally, something to do with, I think, growing up swimming in pools and always being able to see the bottom. When I breathe bilaterally I sort of get a bit dizzy, but right now it's fine, it's great, I'm breathing three to one.

My stroke is strong and clear, the water is cool, and home.

It doesn't disappear, the distance, between one mile and starting, but it… it sort of travels with me. So the route is one mile up, and point four across and one mile back, and that mile, the distance, doesn't vanish, but it also isn't hard.

It's just a thing that I do.

And then suddenly I'm at the buoy where you turn right, and that point four of a mile feels like nothing to the mile that I've just swum up, and then I'm turning again and I'm on my way back. There's a guy with a quite neat stroke who I draft for a little while – drafting is when you sit behind someone in a slipstream and they cut through the water for you. It's not allowed in the biking part of the triathlon, but you can do it in the water, so I do. And then I'm feeling strong, I'm feeling strong, so I sort of pop out and carry on, get ahead of him. Around about half way down that final lap I see to my left, I see the burger vans and the stands and the spectator section and I know, I know, that that's only about 500m from the finish, so then I start calculating the distance I terms that I know.

If it's only 500m, that's 10 laps of Crystal Palace Sports Centre pool. If it's only 400m that's only eight laps of Crystal Palace Pool. There are 300m, that's only six laps, 200m that's only four, 100m, and then there's 50, just one lap of the pool, just one, one length, and I can see the finish line in front of me, and then there are 50 and then there are 25, and then there are 10m to go, and then there is a hand reaching for me and I grab it and someone pulls out of the water. I stop my Garmin and it says 1.05. I've done a personal best. I don't even notice someone grab my wetsuit zip and unzip it for me as I run past. I pull my hat off my head and run to transition. There's a group of marshals there who are shouting at everyone who comes to them, as I pull the wetsuit over my arms. "Just get it over your bum!" I'm like, "What?" "Just push it over your bum!" I'm like, "Okay," and, "Now sit down!" I was like, "What?" "Just sit down!" so I do, and they grab the suit by the arms and the pull it off you. It's amazing. They call themselves 'strippers' and it's the best service I've ever been offered at triathlon, because wetsuits are annoying. I grab my wetsuit and I thank them, and I run into transition. I get my bike gear on and I am feeling good. I've just done a personal best at the beginning of the Outlaw Triathlon!

I put my helmet on, my shoes, I head out, I grab by bike, I get to the mounting point, I climb on, I clip in, and I start spinning.

Next photo

The buzz of the personal best lasts for the first lap of the lake. You then head out; the route is a southern loop of Nottinghamshire, then a line, and then a northern loop, before doing one final southern one and heading back to the water sports centre. I begin my first southern loop. Lots of men in full aero are shooting past me but I choose to think, "How much of a better swimmer must I be to have done better than you in all your aero glory," rather than, "Look at how much of a better cyclist you are."

I feel good. I'm going well. I look at my pace; I've been aiming to hit maybe a 23km average pace, I look down at my Garmin and I'm going 26, 27, 28. And that's not just on the flats as ell – that's an average. I rapidly start recalculating. Obviously I'm going to do a sub 12-hour first full-distance triathlon, that's obviously what's going to happen! So I'm getting really excited and I go through my first feed station really happy – I collect the bottle like a pro and swap it over for my old one. One of the things people don't always know is that British triathlon regulations, they stipulate that you're not allowed to wear headphones at any part of the race, so not only am I going to attempt between 12 and 17 hours of sport, I will do so in the silence of my own head. I don't think in my adult life I am ever alone with myself for that amount of time, uninterrupted, and people often ask me, "What do you do with yourself?" And I actually didn't have an answer until just before. And as part of this process, I worked with a coach, a guy called Simon Ward, who specialises in coaching people via the internet. So he set my training for me, but we also had some one on one face-to-face sessions. And one of the last things he asked me to do was to create a race plan, so he sent through the template and I sort of half had a look at it, and I expected to see like a pace setting, like a physical column, which is all the things you want to be able to be doing physically at each moment – so concentrating on cadence or technique, that kind of thing. And then there was a nutritional column, but the final one I hadn't thought of – and the final one is the one that makes the difference – is the psychological column.

Early on, when I spoke to Dr Sarah Partington, she talked about how difficult it can be to visualise finishing such a long thing, and that visualising is really important for us to achieve things. She talked about setting goals that were shorter; reaching those as a way of getting to that final point. So maybe the longest that you've done is a middle distance triathlon, mark the point in the race where you will have travelled father than a middle distance triathlon, and everything thereafter is a personal best. Think of technique goals, like you're going to hold a certain cadence for a certain amount of time. Simon gave me this race plan template, and on it was a psychological column, and I think of her, and I think of him, and I begin to split my race down into 30 minute sections.

I plan what I will think about for each 30 minutes of the race. So, for example, there is the music half-hour. The music half-hour is me trying to remember – I'm terrible at remembering lyrics – the lyrics to songs that I might know. I will a little personal best prize if I remember all the lyrics to any song. There is only one song, which I end up knowing all the lyrics to, and that is hands Down by Dashboard Confessional, which is an emo song from my youth that's just drilled in from overplaying. I almost get to the end of some *Bugsy Malone* songs because I was in the musical five times as a child, but I don't quite manage it. And I get most of the way through Mambo No. 5 by Lou Vega, which is a good 90bpm cadence to run or swim to, or cycle to as well. So even though I don't 'win' remembering all the words, I do hit a good cadence while I'm trying to remember it.

There's also a maths half-hour, where I count the things around me – the birds and the trees and the clouds – and I make algebra out of them. Or look at the distance that I've gone and try and work it out as a total proportion of both the swim and the cycle, and then the swim, the cycle and the run, or just the cycle itself, and then the percentage that I'd gone of the ride, and then by the time you've done all those calculations the numbers have changed, so you can do them again.

And there's a storytelling half-hour, where I tell myself stories, I daydream a bit. I tell myself stories of falling madly in love or starting the revolution.

So that's what I do with my mind. For the first 60-65km, I'm quite happy – I'm hitting a good pace and I've got an occupied mind. So I end the southern loop, the joining it, I start that, then there's just the bottom of the northern loop of Nottinghamshire to start.

It's not even half way, it's around 80-85km, it's not even half way when the rain starts. The temperature stops as well, it drops to around 12 or 13 degrees – this is a summer day, and it's raining. It starts to rain hard. I've got summer kit on; just shorts and a really light jersey, short-fingered gloves. I've got a gilet with me, but not even a full waterproof. I've got some arm-warmers, which were a last-minute purchase the day before. I put them all on, but it's not enough, nowhere near enough. It's getting cold.

And then that's when the wind starts. 30-40km/h winds. Now, when you're trying to average 23-27km/h, imagine what 40km/h feels like as a wind gust. The land is flat, the wind is sharp and hard, the rain is cold, it stings. My heart rate drops and I start to shiver; I begin to not be able to open the wrappers to my energy bars.

So one of the things that Simon does, my coach, is that he talks in metaphors a lot. I think it's something about having to fit an idea into someone's head in a way that stays with them, even when they've got nothing else left. He says things like, "Hannah, training is like a brick wall: every brick is a training session. If you miss one or two it doesn't matter, the wall is still structurally sound, but if you miss too many, give it a push and it will just fall over." "Hannah, training is like a cake: we've baked the cake, it's a lovely, fluffy sponge. We've put some icing and some jam in the middle, but we haven't put any marzipan over it yet. We haven't put any rolled-out icing on top. We haven't painted anything or added some candles…" he says to me, "Hannah, a race is like life: you get highs and lows. There will be a low point – there's no escaping it in an event of this length, so there will be a point where it is hard, and you feel like you won't be able to carry on. But life, when you have a bad day, you don't give up. You go to be and you get up again thinking tomorrow might be better. You will have lows, but you will have highs again."

Not even half way through the ride, in the biting rain, and the thudding wind, and the cold so hard I can't feel my legs or my fingers- that is my low. I lose the things I was going to do in my head – I can't reach them. The only thing I can do, the only thing I can do is try and raise my heart rate. That's all I can think. So for at least 10 minutes, I spend just trying to pedal faster, increase my cadence to the rhythm, get warm, get warm, get warm, get warm, get warm, get warm. In that time, there is a flicker of memory. I remember that when you don't take on enough carbohydrates to replace what you're using, your body can start to hit the wall, and in the hanging of hormones – in the switching of dopamine and serotonin in your brain – you can actually cause negative thoughts. So I order myself to eat. I stop and I open 2 bars and then put them in my pocket and then I start going again, and I force myself to eat, even though I don't want to, every 5 minutes.

And in the little bit there, in the chanting, and the drinking, and the energy, and the cold, and the biting, biting, heavy… I see Emily.

Seven days before, the weekend before I attempt the Outlaw, I have dinner with my friend at The Bridge pub near Crystal Palace. We have carb-heavy meals and glasses, pints of water. My friend Emily is extraordinary. The day before I attempt the Outlaw, she will set out on the Trans-Continental, a bike race that covers 4,500km. She expect to do it in 10 days.

3 days after my race, I check in with Emily. I look at the site which tracks her via a tracker she wears around her ankle, and I see that not only has she ridden the big climb of the Tour de France, Mont Ventoux, not only has she ridden that, she's ridden it after 24 hours of solid riding, and she has done so in the dark.

My friend Emily is extraordinary. I sit with her, with our high carb meals and pints of water, and I confide in her that I'm scared. I'm scared of meeting my limits; I don't like the idea that I have any. And Emily smiles with her clear blue eyes and she says, "I'm excited. I'm excited about meeting mine, Hannah. Of carrying on anyway."

In the chanting, and the small bit of energy that starts to leech into me, I think of Emily and I come up with a new thing. A new thing to do with my mind. I imagine every single one of the people who wished me good luck. Every single one of the good wishes in the days running up to the Outlaw, in a long line in front of me. I imagine riding up to each and every one of them. I imagine them giving me a push. That gets me past half way. It gets me to 90, then 80 kilometres, and then the maths is friendlier – it's in my favour. There are 70, and then there are 60 kilometres to go, and I am cold, and it is hard, and I still can't feel my fingers, and I get marshals to open energy bars for me, but the maths is friendlier. 60 kilometres!

That's just the same as Beddlestead back to home. And then there are 50, and then there are 40, and that's only Layhams and back, and then there are 30 and 20, and that's not even a commute in London, and then there are 10km to go, and then there are five, and there's a mean little hill, but I get over it, then there are 4, 3, 2 kilometres and a weird sort of stately home that you ride through the back garden of on a road, and there is 1 kilometre to go, and I can hear the crowd, I can hear them! And then there are 500 metres to go, and then there are 400, and I can see transition in front of me, I roll down the hill, and I'm there.

My mum and my brother appear from nowhere – I don't even know how they knew when I was getting in, but they are there, and I am so glad to see them. I say the words, "I'm so cold!" which is exactly when that photo was taken.

A marshal takes my bike from me. I take my helmet off, and I stagger into transition.

I take off my wet clothes, and I cannot tell you how good a pair of dry socks feels until you've gone through that.

The best. Just the best.

I pull on my running clothes and I head out of transition. I start moving.

I'm in the run.

Next photo

And it feels…

… great.

Like, I feel like I'm flying, actually. There's something in the extra amount of exertion it takes to run, which means your heart rate is higher, so suddenly I'm not cold – it's warm.

I'm running, and I can feel my limbs again, and then I'm flying. I check my Garmin and I'm running a 5.30 kilometre. A 5 minute 30 kilometre! That's like my 10k pace! And suddenly I'm recalculating. I could do a four-hour marathon after doing the whole of the Outlaw. I'm recalculating and I'm excited, I think of the way that I'll be able to tell people the story of it. This is the win! This is it.

The loop begins with a lake lap, and then there's an out and back, then one lake, then out and back, then one lake, then one more out and back, and two laps of the lake before finish. I get about 10km in to the 42 that will constitute the marathon. It gets harder. I don't fly through the end of it.

The rain isn't... cruel any more though. It's cooling. And this is when you meet your people. Suddenly... I have quite strong politics, and at the heart of them is the idea of solidarity. A kind of active, doing empathy. In the run is where you find your people. All of you... you've sort of evened out, you find the people who are your pace, who have done your level of training, who have your level of kit. So the people about as good as you are, and they are finding it as difficult as you. I've never felt so surrounded by solidarity, bodily, like I do in the run.

You also chat to people because you're moving slower. There are feed stations where I stop and eat; take on Jaffa Cakes and soggy ready salted crisps and drink flat coke. I walk out of the feed station, for a little while doing a run-walk strategy, and then tell myself, order myself, to start running again afterwards. Around 15-20km in, I meet Chris. Chris has this pace – I see him on the first loop actually, just as he rounds the top of it, of the out and back – and I cross and I see his face, and I see it a couple of times before I actually get around to actually like seeing him and chatting to him. He has this face like (PANTS) the whole way, and it turns out his friend had signed him up without telling him!

Like he told him with some notice, so he'd done the training, but he'd been signed up without his consent.

He had an accent tinted by Newcastle, and we spent some time chatting to one another about the things we'd been depriving ourselves of through training, the things we were going to do after – so I talked about the bottle of Rioja with my name on it, and he talked about the hot bath he didn't care he wasn't going to be able to get out of.

After a while, he decided he decided he needed to walk for a bit and I felt okay sort of running – it didn't really look like a run any more, it was more of a kind of animated stagger – but I decided I wanted to do that for a little bit.

I think there were 10km to go at the point where I met Elliot. Elliot, despite looking on the outside like a broken man, was full of energy when he saw spectators. When someone would say to him, "You're looking strong, man!" He'd go, "Yes! Yes, I am! Thank you! Well done to you!" He just threw it back at people, it was great. By the time I sort of got beside him – we walked through a feed station together and started running – he explained to me that he was a school teacher, which sort of made sense of some of the energy for me. He said he had a little girl, his little girl was in the crowd, and he promised her he was going to do a roly-poly across the line.

He also said that he was doing the Outlaw in memory of a little girl who died at his school in a car accident. They were building a memorial playground with the money that he was raising.

I was one out and back behind Elliot, so I left him to do his final run, final lap of the lake, and then that roly-poly at the end, and set out.

Angela was right. That last bit is just hard. I stop at every feed station, and I take on flat coke, and I walk until I'm done with it and then I drop it in a bin, and I order, I order, I order my legs to move, a kind of half run, half staggering.

I get to the top of the out and back and turn back again. It's raining. It's raining hard. I've given up staying dry; I don't hop around the puddles any more, even if I could find that agility in me, I don't. But the rain feels kind. I watch it pattering across the puddles, and it feels like a blessing, like a benediction. The water is my home, and it's carrying me those last few... few kilometres. I hear the sound swell in the distance as I get closer; I look at my watch and there are 5km to go, and then there are 4, and then there are 3, and I'm back at the lake. I've got 2 laps to go. I do the first lap, and then there are one and a half kilometres, and I spend the top of the final lap just walking from one feed station to the other. Because I'm going to sprint across the line. I don't care what happens, but I am going to find a sprint. I walk steadily and slowly, knowing that I am nearly there, that I can see it now, in a way that I hadn't allowed myself to even try and imagine – I can now actually see the finish line across the lake. I get to that final feed station, I have one Jaffa Cake and a glass of flat coke, I drop the glass and I start to run. There's one kilometre to go, and I pick up speed. There are 800 – and I push myself harder – there are 600 – and somewhere, a long time ago, John is pushing me, and I feel it – there are 500, there are 400, there are 300 metres to go, there are 200, there are 100 – kilo- metres! – in front of me. There are 50 metres, and the crowd is all around me, I'm in the finishing chute, and it feels like nothing, like everything, it feels like the world is around me. There are 25 metres, there are 10, and I think I can hear my brother shouting in the crowd...

I cross the finish line, sprinting.

Someone puts a medal over my head. I stagger around a little, not quite sure where I am, and then someone points to a staircase that leads up to where the spectator area is. There's a handy little sign at the bottom that says GOOD LUCK GETTING UP THE STEPS.

I use a bannister to edge my way up them.

And then they're there. I see them. My mum and my brother, their arms wide open, I fall towards them and they catch me. My mum and my brother stand either side of me and they say, "Well done! Well done!" while I say, "I did it! I did it! I did it!" And they're smiling and laughing and crying, and… I did it.

I did it in 14 hours and 7 minutes.

I completed the Outlaw Long Distance Triathlon.

It was an extraordinary thing, to do… to have done. But I didn't do it on my own.

Back when I was 28, I said it out loud for the first time, and I thought, "It's gonna be mine, my milestone." But this was not just mine, it was ours. It was Sarah's, and her recommendations on visualisations. It was John and his care and inspiration. It was Tom, T-Cass, who showed me the hills of Kent and Surrey. It was Angela, and her email with flat coke and assurances that 'it's just hard but you do it'. It's Phil, and his recommendations on cadence. It's Simon and his race plan and his metaphors. It's Emily and her clear blue eyes as she smiled at the idea of meeting and surpassing her limits. It's Elliot and his roly-poly. It's Chris and his hot bath.

It was my brother, who is called Lawrence.

And there, at the end, like she always is, my mum.

I did it with them. This was our story. Thanks for listening.

Angela Hibbs
20/07/2015

to me

Morning, am sending this at 5am as can't sleep! Legs restless and my quads have disowned me!

Finished in 11hr00m23sec…10th woman, 2nd age group (got the presentation today, Monday) and 102nd overall.

Course was tough and weather really didn't help! V v wet for swim and windy all day, blown everywhere on swim 2nd lap! Glad I used my road bike for the bike… too windy for disc or deep section wheels…overtook loads on the bike, was v wet for first 2 hrs then windy all day, sun then out for end bike and run…too warm!

Felt ok until last 10mikes of run then it got really tough, but you just keep plodding on! Made sure I drank and ate in bike (prob should still have more but felt I did ok)

A tip for you, if there is any…drink the flat coke towards end of run…I started that at 10m to go when started to get sore legs and I think it worked well… or as much as you can hope for! It's instant sugar, but don't do gels as well, yr stomach won't like it.

, I can now plan my tattoo! good luck for yours next weekend! Let me know how u go!!!

Chat to you soon,

Don't think my quads are going to be happy for a few days!

Ang

Hannah Nicklin
20/07/2015

to Angela

Angela this is such a bloody brilliant email to receive! Well done and massive congratulations! 2nd age group! Outstanding!

Such a relief to hear someone I know found it do-able. And the nutrition tip super useful :) flat coke is listed as on all the run stations so that's great (hope there's still some left when I get there ;)

Will definitely let you know how I go.
deep breaths, not long!

Hannah

Sent whilst mobile. All SPaG errors autocorrect related. Honest.

Hannah Nicklin
28/07/2015

to Angela

Hey Ang!

As promised, here's an update on the Ironman!

1) I finished!
2) I SMASHED the swim in 1:05
3) The weather was awful, awful from the second half of the ride onwards. Horrible winds and driving cold rain. You can see it knock 5kmph out of my average speed! And my knees really started hurting - but calves, hamstrings and shoulders previously injured all did well! Took 7,5 hours – LONG
4) I got through the run! Felt amazing for the first 10k because it was just so good to be in temporarily dry clothes, and also to get WARM again. I was so shivery! Then around about half of the marathon in my knees really got tight and I walked for 2-3 minutes out of each aid station. Got through it though! And in 5 hours 10. Sprinted across the line! then hobbled. The coke and jaffa cakes and CRISPS in the run stations were the best. I thought of you a few times, in those last 10 miles 'you just plod through' was in my head quite a bit :)

Doesn't quite feel real!
Overall time was 14 hours 7 minutes… I want to get better on the bike, I think I have a 12.5 hour one in me… I'm sore afterwards! But today I feel a lot better and I travelled back yesterday ok, just some swoops in blood sugar and even small things make me tired! My knees and a weird thing in my foot are sore, but in a sort of 'you worked hard' rather than 'you broke something' kind of way.

My full splits are below if you're interested.

It's been so cool to think of you doing yours, and I'm really proud of us both, for doing it :)

Maybe I'll do a half next year though… get better at the bike and go for another when I'm 32

Thanks again, hope you're doing well afterwards!
Hannah

Split times
Total time   Pos. female   30
34 Split time   Speed split time
2.4mile Swim Swim(Time: 1:05:01) - Pos. 11
Swim   1:05:01 11   4   1:05:01 1:42 min/100m
T1 Transition 1(Time: 9:37) - Pos. 74
T1   1:14:39 16-5   5-1   9:38   -
Bike16M Bike(Time: 7:30:11) - Pos. 107
Bike16M 2:13:39 32-16   6-1   59:00   26.19 km/h
Bike64M 5:10:26 49-17   11-5   2:56:47 26.22 km/h
Bike80M 6:21:37 63-14   13-2   1:11:11 21.70 km/h
BikeTot 8:44:51 81-18   16-3   2:23:14 21.47 km/h
T2 Transition 2(Time: 11:15) - Pos. 86
T2   8:56:06 83-2   16   11:15   -
HPP1 Run(Time: 5:10:59) - Pos. 79
HPP1   9:23:27 79+4   16   27:21   5:51 min/km
ELS1   10:01:28   80-1   16   38:01   6:23 min/km
ERS1   10:11:48   81-1   16   10:20   7:08 min/km
HPP2   11:12:45   78+3   16   1:00:57 6:45 min/km
ELS2   11:59:55   78   16   47:10   7:55 min/km
ERS2   12:11:53   78   16   11:58   8:15 min/km
HPP3   13:24:27   79-1   16   1:12:34 8:03 min/km
Finish 14:07:05   82-3   16   42:38   9:04 min/km

A note from Coach Simon

Now that I'm known as the "Metaphor Man" I shouldn't disappoint with my little paragraph so here it is:

Working with Hannah was like being a sculptor.
When she first contacted me Hannah was like a piece of rough stone.
She had so much work to do and so much to learn BUT I could tell that she had the right mindset.
Over the next few months the stone started to become recognisable as something.
With more work and continued commitment Hannah hit all of her training goals and conquered 140.6 miles of Nottinghamshire countryside to reach the finish line.
Now the rough stone had finally been turned into the unmistakeable shape of an Outlaw triathlete.

A thought from David Lamb, brother of John:

One thing that has struck me when speaking to John's friends is the number of people who he has gently encouraged, pushed on to be better, faster, bolder. It wasn't something I was conscious of at the time, but looking back I can see that he was doing this to me too. The odd terrifying ski run here, a week of early morning running there, drawing something out of you that you didn't know existed.

It's lovely to think that there's this trail of people who, knowingly or unknowingly, have some proud achievement that he helped them to find in themselves.

And as an occasional runner who is acutely aware that I go up almost as much as I go forwards, thank you for providing a little voice in my ear to help me break that habit…

A conversation with my brother, Lawrence Nicklin, about the day of the Outlaw

How did you feel in the run up to it?

I think – it crept up on me the actual event, what I mainly remember is hearing about the training, hearing the numbers and stances and the km you were retelling off before I'd even had lunch at work. So it was mainly that, and I was liking hearing about how excited you were about getting a coach, and how lucky you were to combine your art and your hobby in to one package, but not really being able to conceptualise the distances you were doing, as someone who cycles about 4 miles a day and then back again. The actual event was only really in my head the week before, hearing about your prep was more significant.

How did you feel just before?

All very, very interesting, like none of it was quite how I imagined it would be, on the face of it, like staying where we stayed, that area of Nottingham, didn't look how I expect, it reminded me other places you'd lived, Birmingham I think, I remember looking at you and mum in your different stages of prep stress, what with you also having to do your video stuff too, seeing you systematically tick through your stuff in your head, watching you do your stages and sort of, the way you lean us – and mum for things, and just being not in the way, but I was, ready to do anything you might need us to do, to make life easier, and mum always worries about getting stuff done on time, which is the role you need her to be and obviously she takes it seriously. So actually getting to the place was easy enough, and a relief, it was all dark and cold, unfamiliar. But it was nice to see the lay of the land, as it were, apart from that it was just trying to make life as easy for you as I could. I remember being impressed by the sizes of the crowds that arrived. I was concerned to try and get some good photos. because one person in a black wetsuit and hat and goggles in a crowd wasn't easy. I think, it seemed to me that was when you got into your rhythm of the event, obviously the start's when they pull the starter gun, but you've always taken your preparation seriously, when you can go and fro things useful like arrange your bags in the right order, and check your bike was in order, that seemed part of it for you and you were calm and happy to do that. I think you seemed to be mainly in your own head, working out your strategy, visualising your stroke and rhythm and stuff like that so it's mainly about – just shutting up and letting you get your head straight.

How did you feel during?
The start was quit exciting, they had the emcee, and all the family getting round everyone out on the decks and stuff. The swimming part was quite nice to watch you could see them go all the way up and out and back again, people coming out of the water, people cheering, they had the computer system to pull their names up and people cheered. We saw you come out of the water, but we didn't see you to get your bike, you think we'd recognise you, it was quite frustrating. Your time came up at a check point so we realised. It was good seeing you come out of the water, because obviously that's your event, that's your strong suit, so it was good to see you do well there. You seemed in control, you didn't look too tired, you didn't look like someone had recently tried to dunk you, you look pretty composed. It was kind of pretty happy at that point yeah. Then it was a lot of waiting, a lot a lot of waiting from our point of view, very difficult to time anything with the cycling stage, the check points quite far between, we tried to get on the buses but they were just too full, so we started talking to a Scottish family about sharing a taxi, but the taxi firm quoted ridiculous numbers so me and mum ended up driving out to a garden centre on the route, seeing if we could spot you on the off chance. It started to then hit us quite how long a day it was going to be... because

we got there at 3 didn't we, and that was probably 10 or 11A.M., we'd been up 6 hours at that point and it wasn't even midday at that point.

Then we went back to the place, and took a tour around there, because there were supposed to be Segway tours and outdoorsy events, but there wasn't anything open, so we had a fourth cup of tea and checked out the rapids, the white water rafting stuff. And then we waited at the hill coming down into transition for you based on our estimation of your pace and the last checkpoint, which was a very long wait, but we cheered people as they came in. I watched mum specifically cheering for women, I didn't say anything but I watched her. It started raining, I remember that, we were dressed for it, so it wasn't too bad. I remember having to hide my camera in my coat. I knew I was going to get about 10 seconds warning from when we could make out the people's faces as they came towards us, so it was just being ready for half an hour, and then you turned up and you looked good! You said it was the worst part for you, because of the rain and stuff, and I imagine you were right, but you didn't look – you can tell when someone's done, out of it, exhausted, but you didn't – you looked like I would if I'd done a slightly longer commute to be honest. You were smiling. We saw people fall, we saw people crash at that bit. They ended up telling people to slow down, putting staff up. We saw some people fall on the straight, coming in, that was strange.

And then we caught you coming out of transition into run, which was nice. I put the longer lens on, I saw you smiling, I don't think you saw us, but you were smiling, it's easier to see you when you run, because your gait is more recognisable than your swim or cycle rhythms it was nice you were one the last event because you were doing well, and we'd been up for a while. We went for a walk around the whole park, and then took up position in time for you to be on those last 3 circuits of the lake. I remember feeling strange towards the end because of sitting there, white tired, and the cheering people through, in this weird repetitive, having to cheer, to being tired, but you want, you want people to cheer for your person so you've got to cheer for there person you know. I remember seeing you come down the final carpet, you had a good pace on you, I could tell it was your sustainable pace but you also looked like you had tunnel vision, you were staring at that finish line, all about getting over it, I wished – I guess now I wished we could have got on the carpet with you but it seemed kind of stupid when other people did it. I guess what I wanted to do is be the other end of the finish line. In my mind, days before, thinking about it, we would have been there on the other end of the finish line, to catch you. But there were people everywhere, and security guards, the size of the event. I didn't think you saw us, and I would have liked you to know that we cheered you over the line.

How did you feel after?
Really proud, and kind of hit home what it was like for you because seeing you in your rhythm and your strokes and your pace and stuff, you just looked like you do when you do those things, but seeing you afterwards, you could see how much it had taken out of you, you were pale and your motion was restricted, and you had that exhaustion brain where kind of giddy but also wincing from when you sat on a sore muscle or – not able to really compute things as well as normal so I was happy we got to go with you into that food hall. And see how you managed to pull off the piece to camera even though you were exhausted, quite impressive. Think I remember taking a lot of your weight as we were walking around. I was happy to be able to do that for you.

Did it change how you think about me?
Not that much, because, you pretty much can achieve whatever it is it seems you want to. If someone who'd who I know who's not good at achieving the things they want had

said that, I'd have been very impressed, and I was impressed by the feat you achieved, the intensity of the event, but I think I'd always known you were going to finish, so I was very proud of you and very happy, and like the actual length of times I'd experienced of you doing- obviously I was sat around, but that was while you were cycling – that's longer than I thought someone could do those things for. But I think, if anyone could do it, and you wanted to – you could.

Do you think it shaped us as a family?
I think, it came after that time of change we had with Auntie Iris [dying], so it was off the back of a time when our family roles had shifted slightly, or at least my personal realisation that these roles had shifted, maybe they had been for a while, but mum's always been there for us, to do anything she possibly could to help us, and we've always been proud to be people you can call on… I think I did start to notice mum's stress levels more. Not that she was crazy stressed but like I was just more aware of what she was experiencing, which helped me to take more of a supporting role where in the past I might have just more abled along in the background not realising mum needs me to support her so she could support you. We were both proud of you and proud of us as a group as your family, proud of the family, I guess it felt like, it was more you've been doing sport stuff for a while, but this was bigger, so it wasn't a change of direction for us, but more, we were more proud, more glad to be there for you.

How did you feel about everyone?
It felt like we were the real family. Like you were the only athlete that mattered, and their story wasn't as important a story, their triumph wasn't as great a triumph, it felt nice that there was a race supporting community of – as far as I could see everyone was getting on, everyone was nice to each other, we were a little bit late on cheering people, because it was my first race, and didn't know how it was supposed to be, but we got into that in the end, but this was Hannah's Outlaw.

The strongest memory of the whole day before you finishing was us three on top of the boathouse looking at the sunrise, that was a nice moment for us three, it reminds of a picture I took of you and mum before Leeds triathlon, you looking out over transition with mum hugging you, it was a similar scene, it says a lot about you and mum, that was nice. The concept of not having enough stored calories to finish the race was eye opening for me, in terms of the intensity, it was a physical activity that was impossible without taking food with you – after I told people the crazy distances, the second thing I'd tell them was that fact because that highlights the ridiculousness of it. I remember being annoyed hearing that someone tried to dunk you, that that happened. I liked, I was impressed to see mum on camera, because she was worried about what she would say but then it was 'go' and she didn't flap, there wasn't dead air.

How did you feel leaving me behind.
I was happy that you'd finished, happy that I could tell everyone that you'd done that – slightly worried about you and your journey after that because of your exhaustion, I was looking forward to getting home and sleeping in a bed that fits me. And I guess proud – probably like something that I could never do. So, my attitude for most things in life is I could do it if I wanted to – if I had that time and effort, maybe I could do it and do it better, but it would take me way, way longer or physically my knee would give up… and I wouldn't want to. Heavy frame and all. You could take our body and put it around that and I don't think I could.

Anything to add?
I guess three points come to mind, one is how ridiculous that event is, two that I'm proud to say you completed it, and third one is a non sequitur and I'm aware I sound a lot like dad right now, you know how he talked a lot like this.

A conversation with my Mother, Linda Nicklin, about the day of the Outlaw.

How did you feel in the run up to it?

I always thought you could do it but I wasn't sure at what cost. it was relentless and I knew you'd got lots of help but I did wonder – it's the extreme nature of it, isn't it, it wasn't that I didn't think *you* could do it, I was just worried if you could do it without hurting yourself, and I did wonder if you could ever stop – having got to the level of fitness, and seeing how you were when you couldn't train, you know the endorphins and the release you get from stuff when you work hard like that, how you would ever settle back down to ordinary life. And I trusted the people who were training you and as I said before i had to accept you know more about it than I did, and I had to trust the people who were training you to take care of you.

How you felt just before.

Well that' the only time I can actually really help you with anything because you require me to help you with the logistic and to be there to support you, so it's important to me to get it right and I don't always know if I can do it, or I worry I might spoil things by getting it wrong, it feels like massive responsibility to get you there on time, but it's also the least I could do, so I did worry I won't be able to get you there on time, and I also know that if I don't cope I'm getting in the way of your mental preparation, but Lawrence was helpful, it's a big responsibility for me. We would have worked something out, but it's the worry isn't it, and I don't mind getting there early. I didn't mind we were the fourth car there or something. But I do find that part stressful. Did I sleep on the settee? I did didn't I. It's about being there to support you but not getting in the way.

And if you want to go and do something four times, go through bags or whatever, that's fine, because it's part of your mental preparation. Getting there in the dark, and then a really cold crisp dawn, which we knew would be the best part of the day because the weather was due to get nasty. Getting to the location wasn't difficult, but it could have been. And then walking around there and nothing had really started yet. I'm confident that you'd remembered everything, I remembered trying to work out how to get to where I could see well. Nothing being open. And waiting a long time for it all to start, hoping that you've got it in you to do it. I didn't want you to meet your – find your limit and it not work out, bothered how you would make a performance out of it all. It would have been hard if you'd had to stop for some reason. Then trying to work out where to be at different time. It was cold. I wish I'd taken more clothes. It was a surprisingly cold day. I couldn't see where we'd go, but I didn't want to leave. But we had to drive about to charge the phone, to continue tracking you, on the phone.

How did you feel during?
The water part I didn't want you to get kicked in the face, but I knew it was your element, and you enjoy swimming in the water, and what you got started you'd be fine. Pretty difficult to spot you in that mass of people, so it was hard – you changed your stroke a bit, you learnt how to do that free water stroke, I didn't doubt for a second that you could do that, and that you were probably enjoying it, so the other things was to look for someone with your kind of a stroke, but there's always how to get you out the water, because we seen ones where people fall over on the way out. And you did a really good time didn't you – you always tell me the time you think you're going to do – and then you beat yourself…

Another problem is you don't have your phone on you, so I have to trust the race organisers to make sure you're OK.

Any other time, if you go out, and there's a problem, then you can call me. I didn't know the route to drive to come and find you. And you can't call. Once you're out the water, on the bike and on the roads, it's up to the race organisers to look after you, keep you safe, and that's a bit hard. I remember seeing you run round. I'm not a very enthusiastic cheerer, I feel silly shouting, I wait until you run past and say 'come on Hannah you're doing fine' rather than shouting from a distance. We missed you – saw you going in but don't think we saw you leaving, because that was part of the problem of knowing where you were. You were tracked, chipped, that's how we ran down our phones. And while you were out on your bike the weather took a turn for the worse, we hadn't trained for standing in the rain for 12 hours, perhaps we should have done. It wasn't as if we were walking about, and the facilities were heaving with people.

So when you were out on your bike we did drive about a bit and try and work out where you were. We went to a garden centre, and also to charge the phone, but we couldn't get anywhere to where you were. Because I thought you would be finding that difficult because it was very windy then, and I wanted to cheer you on. So we went back to the turn, by transition, because that was the best spot to say hello, but I think not having seen you leave we weren't confident what kit you had on. So we were pleased to spot you there. You looked absolutely fine, but you said you were absolutely freezing, but then we'd seen lots of other people and you looked just as good as everybody else, you didn't look harmed by it, you know. But as you came past you sad you were absolutely freezing, and I know you have in the past, your feet have gone dead, so I'm not the slightest bit surprised but it was just astonishment you'd managed to keep going that long and travel all that distance, and then wondering how on earth you were going to manage to do a marathon. Except through sheer force of will… and training.

You were out ages at that point. We did go out to the canoe place and watch the white water bit… there were long gaps where we walked about. Saw you coming out and off into the run, and from that point it was a loop, a circuit we could move about – so we could position ourselves because at one point we knew you were where you were, so we could walk with you, there was a piece by the lake, we walked back to where you'd last been marked so we knew we would bump into you – so we tried hard to see you at different points. It went on a long time, I thought you were further ahead. That marathon was long, and the commentary was tedious. "You are an Outlaw" to everybody who came over. It's always nice to see the community and the families that are supporting you, and the types of people who do it, if you saw them in the street, it's something in their minds that makes it possible, because there's nothing in their shapes – all shapes and sizes, very admirable things that people do.

I've got a bit of video of you finishing, because – they were calling you out because we'd already spotted you because we know what you look like when you run. We saw you when you only had one lap to do, so we just, stood by the crossing line, very proud of you. I don't know how you did it -you kept running right to the end, there was no slowing down. Do you remember feeling dizzy in the tent? I'd had words with one of the guys who was stopping people coming up the steps to meet the athletes… so when you got dizzy, I wanted to go into the food tent and he wanted to stop me, but he didn't. I remember being incredibly proud of you, just keep going to your limits that whole time. Very proud of you, and pleased that the three of us were together, that support, we'd each done our bit. And then thinking what the hell's next. Hope you don't want to run across some desert or something, because I couldn't do the logistics of that.

How did you feel after?

Very happy, very relieved, concerned that you – because you had a full day planned the next day, and deadlines. When you did the Lake District one, when you finished that, you were having difficulty walking, you didn't have time for that to happen. So I was immensely proud of you but concerned. We moved stuff around the flat so you could get out if you couldn't move in the morning. Because when you did the one in the Lake District, watching you trying to walk to the train afterwards, you don't make things easy for people to help you. I just didn't want any of those things to happen. I didn't know if you would be able to get down the stairs of that apartment. You ask a lot of yourself. So I was pleased and happy everything had gone as well as it could, so everything was just how were you when we left you. If you'd been coming home I could have watched you, to see if you were alright, but I couldn't do that. But the dosage time it was late and we had to be getting on. You were pleased with your times I think that you were exhausted. You didn't seem injured – and your preparation had work out well, except for that you'd got so cold. When – there's not a lot of room for me to be doing mum things because you've got everything planned down to the last atom. If I'm being mumsy I'm getting in the way. Quite a hard balance. Because you also need support.

Did it change how you think about me?

I suppose my respect for what you can actually achieve went up a notch. I do think you work your body like a machine, and there's more to a body than a machine, and I wonder what on earth you'd do when it didn't work like a machine. For instance when you hurt your shoulder – like the one who stopped because she only had one more run in her – what on earth you'd do then. But I'm very proud of you.

Do you think it's something to do with us as a family?

Me, you and Lawrence are a good team and I was proud that – when we have common goals we're very good at meeting them, we're maybe not always agreeing about how one of them does a thing, but when the decision's made, we do them. I don't want to take away from your achievement but – and I'm proud of what you and Lawrence mean to each other.

How did you feel about everyone?

I kind of talked about that – that the, all kinds of people, every kind of people that you might expect, and all of their motivations for doing it are admirable, and just the – I don't think that when I was growing up, the closest we got to doing, cross country was probably as close as I got at school, and I used to skive off them… the route was past my house, so we used to peel off, me and my friends used to just go in and have a cup of coffee, and catch them on the way back. We made sure we never did a personal best or something, but we didn't come in last either. My mother did wonder where the coffee used to go. So it's not exactly in my history to have the determination to do the these things you choose to do. I didn't grow up – I don't know other people who have that kind of commitment and determination, so its very good, and the reasons why people do them, the causes people are supporting makes me feel quite — I admire the people who translate something that's been a difficulty in their life and make a positive thing about it. Nice to see the teams supporting one another, because it's about a personal best, isn't it, in some ways the well-oiled machines are less admirable to me than the ordinary people doing extraordinary things. Because the well-oiled machines are young men who will just grow old like the rest of us, whereas the people just like us are the ones doing something brave. The amount of time that families contribute to it, it's never a one-sided thing, for every hour someone's out training there's someone else looking after the kids.

What do you think about (endurance) sport?
I think that – sports, I think you feel better about your body when you're doing sport, and I like to think of you being strong and healthy and doing good things not just with your mind, because it would be easy for you to just be in your mind, I think sport is a good balance. I like doing things, I don't think I – I think sport, exercise is necessary, sport is how you make exercise fun, I guess. And I know that you find swimming and things calm your mind so are really important in your life. It's important women do sport, and do it in a way that's – and then that's not judgemental, it's easier for women to feel looked at, be put off by it. Like I've got a friend who's happy to play golf, so long as she doesn't get sweaty or wet. It's good to be aware of the physical body that you inhabit, because only then can you keep it properly healthy and be balanced in your life. Because if it's invisible, it's just the locomotion that gets your mind to where it needs to be, there's a whole load of joy missing in your life, and you won't be ultimately healthy and you'll have limitations.

Why do you think I did it?
I think that there's the whole piece of art thing, the performance, but that kind of fixed you in the commitment to do it, it was a major motivation, but you did a mini triathlon, and then a triathlon, and then it wasn't enough – like doing your PhD, you wanted to go to the limit. Ironman is up there. And because you enjoy it? And it's this thing about meeting your limits as well, a mental game.

Anything to add?
I think that's about it. Proud of you – said that haven't I? It's an expensive business. Makes it hard to feed you when you're in training. And I always want to be there. There'll be times when I can't support you at a race and I'll be sad about that.

An excerpt from my interview with Phil Hayes, sports scientist at Northumbria University

HN: Why do we train?

PH: So there's a really good quote from a guy called David Costill who was an exercise physiologist who was probably the most prominent person through the 1980s. And he did lots of stuff on running and then got into swimming in his later career. And he said 'The purpose of training is to stimulate growth, growth only occurs with periods of rest and recovery'...which I really like because it tells you everything about training you have to work hard to get the body to adapt and grow and you also need to have periods where you rest and recover to allow those changes to take place because...if you just work hard all the time eventually everything breaks down. So I like his quote because it gives you all of what the process is. We train to grow and adapt, and the things that grow and adapt are the structures in the body, so within the muscles, the muscle structures change, within the heart the heart structure changes, the blood vessel structure changes, and because of those structural changes we then get a change in the way our body functions.

HN: Tell me about the structural changes.

PH: So in endurance training there are two areas of adaptation, one is the central cardiovascular system so your, the ability of the heart to deliver blood and therefore oxygen to the working muscles and the other changes are within the working muscles and their ability to use the oxygen they get. In terms of delivery it's about the heart getting bigger, stronger, so with every beat it pumps out more blood.

HN: Cos the heart is a muscle.

PH: Yes that's right, yes, so the heart itself, we measure the output by recording something called cardiac output which is heart rate plus the amount blood per beat, which is called stroke volume, so heart rate times stroke volume gives us the cardiac output which me measure in litres of blood per minute.

That's how much blood is circulated round the body per minute, so that goes up because the ventricle of the heart, the capacity of the ventricle gets bigger and the muscle gets stronger depending on what training you do and performance but essentially that's what happens. So we're able to pump more blood around the body and then the working muscles themselves get more blood vessels that supply them, so there's more capillaries supplying them and so more oxygen getting delivered so inside the muscle cells you, so they're the part of the muscle cell where the oxygen is used, the enzymes associated wit breaking down fats and carbohydrates increase and then the end product of that which reacts with the oxygen so the amount of oxygen we get we're able to you are bale to provide more energy from aerobic sources.

HN: Energy is made in itself of mitochondria…and they do that by taking oxygen.

PH: They take either it can be glucose, it can be fat, they break them down into small particles which eventually interact with the oxygen, and then that will then be productive of energy.

HN: So you can't get enough oxygen to match, that's anaerobic.

PH: It's, not quite, that's a popular misconception, the carbohydrate breaks down and then the end product of carbohydrate breaking down is called pyruvate, and that then either converts to lactate or enters the mitochondria, so the rate at which you produce pyruvate it becomes a logjam if you like, the mitochondria moving fast enough which doesn't seem to be dependent on oxygen availability, certainly not once you get going maybe at the first onset of exercise it might do but it's like a sink and the rate at which you break down carbohydrates is like turning the tap on in the sink, and all you're doing is putting more plugholes in the sink to drain the water…that would be the analogy I would use, I suppose so the faster you run the faster you're letting the water out the tap and so it either drains away or it builds up…part of that build up will be associated with products… and you reach a level where you have to stop so if you have more plugholes you can allow a faster flow of water before it pools up and you have to stop.

HN: So training, exercise getting used to it, it forms…

PH: Yeah essentially you produce more mitochondria, you get more and they get bigger.

HN: So you're able to drain more pyruvate.

PH: So it's not so much about there's more so you can process more so much as there are more so they drain quicker, they drain the pyruvate quicker and therefore the bad effects like the build up of lactic acid.

HN: Lactic acid.

PH: …That happens later on.

So lactic acid build up is sort of dependent on the intensity of exercise so if you are untrained and you go out and you do a run or say you run on a treadmill at different speeds the point at which lactic acid built up to the level where you would need to stop would be quite early.

HN: Why does it stop you?

PH: Well for a number of reasons, the ideas are changing here, and I know you've got a question later so there is a complexity about what goes on Partly from the idea of changing gear, so… I suppose the traditional part is you make the muscle acid so part of the lactic acid is you get some build up of acids and that inhibits partly the bits where force is produced in the muscle and partly slows down the rate at which you produce energy so slowing down the tap it becomes self-regulating system.

But there are people now who are contesting that view and the view is a bit undecided but we don't think the acid is produced where they originally said it was. There are…that's a contestable point, perhaps, but the traditional view is that's what happens. As you get fitter, as you get aerobically fitter you produce more mitochondria so the speed at which you reach the point where that lactic acid starts to build up is going to be faster so you are then able to run for a longer period of time, run at faster speeds before you reach that point. So that's how you make progress in your running, you are able to run for longer times… And also within the muscle you are able to break down fats more so you spare your carbohydrate store so if you are doing something like a triathlon where it's a long period of time you saving your carbohydrate stores and relying more on fat to produce some of that energy so you are potentially prolonging your capability. You could fatigue, not because of lactic acid build up from an intensity thing but if you're in a triathlon. You're more likely probably to fatigue because you've run out of carbohydrate.

HN: And that's why you're supposed to eat every half hour?

PH: Yeah, yeah. So the classic running out of carbohydrate is the runner hitting the wall. That's the prime example of what happens. So you running out of carbohydrate and then you have to depend on fat metabolism and fat metabolism is slower than carbohydrate metabolism so you have to go at the speed at which you can produce energy from fat. So... So classically you end up walking or very slow jogging. So by having more mitochondria you spare those carbohydrate stores and so potentially you can go for longer.

HN: Angela was saying it's more efficient to burn fats, not efficient, what was the word she used so the value of burning fat is higher than carbohydrates.

PH: Right.

HN: She probably said the right thing I just told you the wrong thing.

PH: So there's an increased oxygen cost associated with burning fat and burning carbohydrate...helped by an efficient fuel to burn but we don't have much of it so it's so yeah there is...by burning fat we spare the limited carbohydrate sources we have. So for example we have fat as a store because it's a very efficient way of storing energy... so for every gram of fat we get 9 calories of energy and for every gram of carbohydrates we get 4 calories of energy so that's why we have fat stores rather than carbohydrates stores, if you had carbohydrate stores your bodyweight would increase enormously. So it's a very effective way of storing large amounts of energy.

HN: Yeah.

PH: So think the figures of a 70kg man if they didn't have fat stores but had carbohydrate stores would weigh like 105 kg or something... So clearly it's a very efficient mechanism. So breaking down the fat and using the fat has quite high energy cost or higher energy cost than using carbohydrates, but it's sparing the limited resources you have for the carbohydrate.

HN: So if you were to have a constant and exactly measured to you and your genetics and circumstances supply of carbohydrates and you were on a treadmill and you ran and ran and ran does that ever, does that, what are then the limiting factors, is it then oxygen?

PH: Well no…

HN: Can you go on forever?

PH: I suppose theoretically you probably could; you'd probably dehydrate and then there would be the need to sleep, there would be the need to stop and go to the loo, there's a whole range of other things, but yes, there would be lower intensity if you didn't need to eat. Sleep, whatever you could technically you could theoretically keep going…yeah. So yeah low level exercise theoretically could keep going providing the fuel and hydration you could keep going kind of constantly.

HN: So it's not our muscle it's our fuel.

PH: Well, I mean, I suppose the traditional view of running performance has been metabolic and so you stop because you run out of energy or the waste products from high intensity exercise build up so we've had that view of metabolism being the limiting factor, but I would imagine that you couldn't, you know, keep going forever because you'd get muscle damage, so I think there are other things but that area is relatively poorly investigated.

An excerpt from my interview with Sarah Partington sports psychologist at Northumbria University.

SP: Why don't I start with a little bit about the Storied self and what I mean by that and it's something that I explored in my PhD studies and it actually dovetails quite nicely with the things you've been talking about because my PhD was around flow and intrinsic motivation and why do people do the things that they do and in trying to understand that I was actually, trying to tap into getting people to talk to me about the sort of experiences they d had and why they were so engaged in them and one of the things that I realised was that, in trying to communicate to me about their own personal experiences, they were trying to tell stories so I mean you just told me your story and you put it into a recognised story format and that's one of the things we know that that people do and in studying it, it's linked to how we make sense of ourselves and our identities and how we communicate those identities to ourselves but also to other people. So the stories that we tell, the stories that we construct are very personal stories but they are also social stories because we share them with others.

Now one of the things I explored in my research – and there's a wider research network around these kind of concepts is how we create our identity through stories and really the idea that we try and make sense of who we are, how we became who we are, why we do what we do. By creating a story around it, to create a sort of coherent sense of self. So we almost look back on instances from our past in the way you've just done and we try and create a coherent story around that in order to put the pieces together to say this is me, this is who I am, this is what I'm about this is how I understand myself and this is how I'm going to communicate who I am to you and we put them in that kind of recognised storytelling format so that other people can understand them and can engage with them and also either accept or reject them.

So, y'know, if we re trying to claim a certain identity, yes we can claim but it has to be validated by other people. SO you know, your identity I'm a swimmer, this is who I am, I'm going to tell stories around swimming. But other people also have to accept you as a swimmer for you to be able to claim that identity but the story that you tell will also be structured by the stories that you hear, so you will have heard other swimmers telling their stories, now you'll have heard other triathletes telling their stories, other sportsmen and women and we map not them the stories that we hear and the sort of social discourse to try and create our own stories that are coherent to us and also make sense to others. So the technical terminology of it from the literature is basically narrative maps but really it's just sort of familiar stories that, dominant narratives that we about examples from sport would be like no pain, no gain or the stories of the underdog, winning against the odds and if you look into the research you'll find that academics are trying to classify them you find they'll call it the restitution narrative, which is really the comeback story for example you know and er, I've overcome adversity sort of common story in sport so a lot of time when people are talking about their own identity as a sportsman or woman they may link on to that kind of story to try and make sense of who they are and just to have that kind of identity communicated and recognised as a sports man or woman but not just to other people but to themselves I think so that they can understand themselves and make sense of who am I, what's me and you know where's home? Things that you automatically described when you were, at the start of this, telling me your story.

HN: So is there evidence that there is benefit for, the people who can tell themselves the best stories about themselves, are they better sports people?

SP: Not necessarily in terms of better sports people but in terms of the sort of social status that would go around with it be that the acceptance the kudos you might get, the recognition. We know that there are benefits associated with having a highly functioning performing body, referred to in literature as the gloried self, y'know it's 'cause you get that kudos from having a body that will perform. SO that in combination with, if you are unable to tell those kind of stories, stories that people are interested in and want to hear about again and it kind of creates this Gloried self. This feeds back because you kind of get the recognition you get the acknowledgement you feel good about yourself and that identity is validated.

HN: And I suppose a story must be the fallen hero because that's kind of the Oscar Pistorius or Lance Armstrong as well.

SP: Yes there are a variety of stories that we hear and there are some stories that we don't hear so you were talking about women, previously women in sport. Sometimes women's stories don't get heard and just linking to some of the issues around gender and sport – I won't go into that in massive detail as that wasn't my specific area of research but we do know that some stories and some narratives are more dominant than others and if you want to be hear sometimes you have to tell your story in a particular way to be heard. It may no be the natural way you that you would like to tell your story, people tend to adapt their stories so that they can so that they can have the stage really to tell them. In ways that are recognisable and acceptable.

HN: Okay so, does that mean that like, bringing that into a really specific context of starting out on a big piece of endurance sport in a competition context, in a smaller level being able to tell the story to yourself of succeeding, of like visualising yourself crossing the finish line, that kid of thing, telling yourself stories about that is that like per formatively helpful?

SP: Yeah so, it's starting to build that identity and sense of self that belief, it's almost creating a new identity – something that you've done from scratch – so it's starting to build the self-belief the way you talk about yourself, the way you think about yourself and we do know that the way people think and the beliefs that they have can actually shape the way in which they behave. There's a kind of link between what you re thinking, how you feel, how you perform and how you behave and you know, we're sort of linking now into sport psychology and some of the key techniques a sports psychologist might link into. Being & the awareness of thoughts, gaining cognitive control over the kind of thoughts you are having and being aware of how those thoughts do make you feel can shape the way in which you behave. Thoughts are very powerful and it doesn't just have to be thoughts it can be visual images as well, a lot of the work sport psychologists do is around visualising. Imagery is extremely popular, a lot of people think imagery is about recreating experiences but it doesn't have to be recreating it can be about creating new experiences or experiences that have never happened. So being able to visualise yourself successfully coping or successfully achieving has been – indicating the literature that it can help in terms of improving performance.

HN: So I sent you a video – a really famous video – of a woman right at the end of an Ironman. One of like the early ones in the 90s, literally just falling to the floor and getting up and falling to the floor then getting up then falling to the floor again and then just crawling to the finish line. Why do we do that why not just stop?

SP: I know, from a psychological perspective I don't think there's any simple, easy answer as to why we do what we do I mean there's various levels of behaviour and obviously that one stands out as being quite extreme and anyone who's watched it, it's actually painful to watch isn't it and you almost want to just make it stop and logically as a human being, you re sitting there thinking why don't you stop and I think part of it is – we did try and talk about getting people motivated to be engaged in physical activity and for most of the general public – it's almost the opposite – we re trying to actually get them to engage to a certain level to even do something and then you get people who are engaging at such a level that it almost becomes damaging to their health, anybody watching that and as I say it a painful experience to watch, there are multiple theories out there around what motivates us to initiate a behaviour and to continue to maintain that behaviour. Which can be different reasons so different reasons for starting a behaviour so you might have had different reasons when you started it to what's actually maintaining your behaviour now. And there are all sorts of theories out there and models we can try and use to understand it. I still don't think we've got enough clarity to be able to say this one theory can explain such a complex environment.

I suppose at various different levels it initially you might talk about intrinsic motivation so this is where flow comes in that there is a mental state that encourages where the athlete, the athlete becomes so involved or so engaged in the activity that they lose that awareness of self, they lose the awareness of what else is going on around them and it is just then the activity and they re in that moment and they can't actually they just don't have that awareness of what's going on around, outside them. Flow is usually described as an extremely positive optimal psychological state however if you go back to the early research there are warnings about how flow can become addictive. So you know it's so absorbing and it's so involving that perhaps we can then start to really get engaged in the activity to the detriment of everything else. It becomes all encompassing now I don't know whether that would explain what we've seen in that clip but flow may explain how people can become so involved in some activities that they cannot stop and they do keep going even though you know everyone would be screaming at them to please stop, please stop what you re doing. So you know autotelic activity when they get to that stage where the activity is so rewarding in and of itself it's difficult to describe that because I that it comes down to something very personal for that individual and that particular activity in that specific moment.

A lot of time we're doing activities that and well we talked a lot about before, mastery was one that you mentioned I think that you mentioned in your story at the beginning and some of the key theories that we talk about around self-determination theory, personal growth and actualisation and partly it's that you set yourself these goals and to achieving these goals and you really do get self-fulfilment as you get those mastery experiences. Self-determination experts would talk about a sense of autonomy and agency and purpose so you know you've had this free choice and you are engaging in something that you have chosen to do for a purpose that is important to you and the other part of that theory would be about connectedness, maybe connected to a broader you know, social network outside of you or something bigger so I guess for you it would be about feeling like part of that Ironman fraternity, that you reconnected to something that's bigger than just you, there's a social group and a social identity beyond your personal identity. And I suppose again, this sort of self-actualisation it's again very reinforcing. I suppose it may back fire in terms of, you keep pushing and keep pushing and keep pushing and it becomes very difficult and if you've set your heart on these particular goals and that is part of you identity to then not complete the goal could actually shatter your identity. So again I don't know,

I don't know if that would explain that type of behaviour but I suppose that if we pull across all the different theories that, that are out there we could look at it, it may become autotelic it may have some elements of self-determination in there and it may be linked to an identity and if you aren't able to maintain this goal or this competence that drives you, it's really like your identity is going to be shattered it becomes so important that you can't fail, you have to keep going no matter what.

An excerpt from a blog post (soon to be a book) by Emily Chappell, about her experience of the Transcontinental bike race.

Transcontinental: Night on bald mountain

Ventoux needs little introduction, but in case you're one of the few non-cyclists who read this blog, you should know that it's one of the most iconic climbs of European cycling, notorious for claiming the life of British Tour de France rider Tom Simpson in 1967 (though alcohol and amphetamines also played a part); feared for its unrelenting gradient and the fierce winds that roar around its upper slopes (the clue's in the name: *venteux* = 'windy'); famous for being really really hard, no matter *who* you are. In marked contrast to all the other difficult climbs I've ridden over the years, it's not a pass (the lowest possible route through a mountain range) – it's a peak. The road winds its way across the barren limestone landscape, all the way to the very top. It's a folly, in many senses. It won't get you anywhere. There's no reason to go up there other than to destroy your legs and admire the view. Otherwise, if you really needed to be on the other side of it, it would take far less effort (and probably not much more time) to take a longer route around its base.

Attempting a climb like this for the first time you'd want to be fresh, and well rested. You'd want to have spent the previous evening carb-loading, followed by a good night's sleep, you'd want to be wearing clean shorts (or perhaps even brand new ones), you'd want to be in a good mood, energetic, raring to go, excited about what lay ahead. I was none of these things.

Deprived of the catharsis and comfort of seeing Juliana, I found there was nothing left in me but exhaustion, and knew already that this was a deeper tiredness than could be remedied by a square meal and an hour or so of sitting around. But there was nothing else I could do. 'I'll rest and eat' I told myself, 'then I'll make a start on the climb.' Put like that it sounded like a plan. But I knew it would take more than that. What I needed was a day off. Maybe a week off. I was finished. But I couldn't be – I still had over three-quarters of the race ahead of me. And Ventoux. I hadn't even *got* to the hard bit yet.

There didn't seem to be many restaurants in Aubignan, and the ones I did find weren't open yet. I did a couple more torturous circuits of the town, looking for something I could eat, but even the supermarket was closed. Eventually I settled for a bar where the waitress had told me they started serving pizza at 6P.M. – still half an hour off, but what did it matter? There was nothing else I could do with that time. I'd have to climb Ventoux in the dark (despite my optimistic projections of the previous night), but since the climb currently looked impossible anyway, one more element of difficulty didn't seem to make much difference. I sat myself down on the outside edge of the terrace, remembering that the waitress hadn't smiled at me as I walked in, worrying that I wasn't welcome, with my dishevelled appearance and sweaty lycra, trying to calculate how long it had been since I last had a shower (76 hours), since I last washed my hair (130 hours), wondering how bad I really smelt, since I was largely oblivious to it myself.

The pizza I eventually ate wasn't anywhere near enough. I could have had the same again, but I feared the waitress's disapproval. I settled for a plate of tiramisu, and as much water as I could drink. I didn't feel any better for eating. Maybe there was nothing for it but to give in and sleep for a while. I still had about 20km to go before I started the climb, and the heat was beginning to drain out of the day as the shadows lengthened and the sun sank over the luminous Provençale landscape. I got back on my bike, telling myself that I could stop any time I wanted to, that perhaps a couple of hours' snooze in a field might sort me out. But I knew that it would probably have as little effect as the pizza I'd eaten. I might as well just carry on, and quit delaying the inevitable. I stopped at a fountain in Caromb and threw water over my face and arms and legs. It didn't help. I stopped in Bédoin and drank an espresso. It didn't help. The mountain loomed over me, its peak still glowing with the light of day while shadows fell everywhere around me.

It's difficult to explain what I was feeling as I pedalled slowly towards the start of the climb. I wasn't afraid – I hadn't the energy for such grand, decisive emotions. Instead I had a sense of what lay ahead of me being impossible, but also inevitable. There was no way of avoiding this, and at the same time I knew that I hadn't the strength to see it through. But nor did I have the imagination to find any better solution than just carrying on. So carry on I did, through the outskirts of Bédoin, past its low stone walls and olive groves, under an apricot sky in air that smelt of lavender.

Km 1-4 – Hannah

As I turned onto the road that would lead me up to the summit of Ventoux I felt something break inside me. It was nothing like you might imagine – nothing like I myself had imagined when speculating on what terrible things might happen to me during this race. Nothing snapped, or cracked, or shattered. Instead it felt more like melting; a gentle, delicate collapse, like a body falling exhaustedly into sleep after a long day's work, like a final, blessed surrender. I felt myself start to cry, but in a way that was more a merciful release of tension than the expression of pain.

I had been here before, just once in my life, and always wondered when I might go back. The day after I finished my 11-day dash through eastern China in 2012 (riding over 100 miles a day to beat a visa deadline; at that point the hardest ride I'd ever attempted) I stepped off the ferry in Incheon and started to ride the 50km to Will and Julie's house. Normally this would take me less than 3 hours. That day it took me 12. I got lost. Impossibly lost. For hours and hours, as the sky darkened around me and the rain came down, I pedalled exhaustedly through the edgelands and industrial areas of Seoul and Incheon, following signposts that led me persistently round in circles, backtracking again and again, frequently despairing that I would *ever* find a way out of this nightmare. Having slept through most of the ferry crossing, I had more-or-less forgotten that I was significantly depleted by my exertions in China, but this must have had something to do with the fact that, eventually, I just broke down.

I have always been anxious to stop myself from crying in situations like this, imagining that if I give in to the tears then it's all over, and I've failed, and the final remnants of strength and resolve that I was trying to hold onto will be swept away in the ensuing tide of salt water. But sometime late that evening I ran out of the strength I was using to hold them back. Sheltering under a bridge next to the Han River, I sobbed out loud for a few minutes, not caring who saw or heard (though there was no one really about). Then I made a discovery that surprised me: this wasn't the end after all. I got back on the bike, and I carried on pedalling. And crying. My sobs were gentle, soft, calm, almost like breathing. For half an hour or so I cycled along weeping quietly to myself; then my mood shifted, the rain stopped, and I finally found myself on the right track.

I turned this episode over in my head afterwards. I'd heard that pushing yourself hard on the bike could have strange effects – friends who'd done long Audaxes had reported hallucinations after riding for 24 hours without sleep – but I'd never known there was a crying stage. 'It'll be easier next time,' I told myself. 'Last night I thought I was going to lose it. Next time I'll know it's just the crying stage.'

Three years later, here I was again, at the crying stage. A couple of tears ran down my cheeks, and a few sobs escaped my lips, quickly dying down into whimpers. Any resistance I had left in me melted away. I hadn't broken, I realised; I had dissolved. And yet somehow I was still here, still cycling. I thought about an email a friend had sent me the previous day, in response to some of my enthusiastic burbling about how much fun I was having cycling through France.

> I love that you're loving it. If you stop loving it (or have a moment where it becomes type 3 fun) I'll still love that. Basically, it seems you can do no wrong.

This wasn't the first expression of unconditional love I've ever received, but it was one of the few I've managed to take to heart.

'It doesn't matter!' I thought to myself, feeling as if I'd discovered some life-changing secret (which perhaps I had). Suddenly I knew what I should have known all along: that all of these pointless challenges I flog myself through are unnecessary and irrelevant. I am already enough. I am already admired. I am already loved. Perversely, rather than removing any incentive to carry on, this realisation boosted me forward. Perhaps it was because I knew that I no longer had to grit my teeth, gird my loins and grind my way up the mountain, muscles bulging and sweat pouring, constantly wrestling with the urge to give up and the weight of everything I had to prove. There was no more conflict here. All I had to do was keep going. It didn't matter how slow I was. I didn't have it in me to race up Ventoux like the hero I wished I was (like I imagined all the men had done), so there was no sense in trying. I could choose to stop, or I could choose to keep going, and if I kept going then I wouldn't be breaking the promises I'd made to myself when I entered this race back in November.

I thought about Hannah Nicklin, a relatively new friend of mine, and someone I already massively admire, who just the day before had completed her first Ironman triathlon. We had met for lunch in Crystal Palace the previous week (how long ago that seemed now!), to discuss our respective challenges, and our fears, and our coping strategies. Hers were far more developed than mine.

Sitting at a picnic table in a sunny pub garden, with plates of carbohydrate and glasses of tap water between us, she told me about the race strategy she had written; how she had divided the 3.8km swim, 184km cycle and 42km run into 28 half-hour segments; how for the run she had even planned in advance what she was going to think about during each segment, in order to keep herself on track.

I'm going to spend one half hour trying to remember all of the songs that I actually know the words of [...], another half hour will be spent counting, turning the world around me into algebra. Then there's a daydreaming half hour. One small half hour where I get to dream about saving the world and falling madly in love and starting the revolution. Another half hour is the half hour of breathing. Measuring breath to step, and listening carefully to all the sounds around me.

I listened to her, impressed by how thorough and methodical her preparations were. If anyone asked me about my own strategies for when things got difficult (and one or two people already had), all I could offer was some vague mumbling about having done a lot of cycling before, and often found myself at the point where I thought I couldn't go on, and always somehow muddled through. I had a certain amount of faith in my own resilience, without ever having bothered to think through how this resilience actually *worked*, and what its limits might be. But I doubted I would ever plan out my race experience as meticulously as Hannah had hers. It just wasn't my style.

Now I changed my mind. It is 21km to the summit of
Ventoux from the start of the climb, and I still knew that that
was impossible in my current state. But if I divided the climb
into segments of two kilometres… That wouldn't be so bad.
I had already ridden half a kilometre or so just thinking it all
over, almost without noticing. So if I could find something
to think about for each segment – something to focus my
mind on, to distract me from the impossibility of what I was
trying to do, to mask my weakness and cushion my fear – all
I would have to do is ride for 2 kilometres, stop, rest, stretch,
drink, and then ride for 2 more. I could do that. I hoped.

Instinctively, I knew what would spur me on. I decided that
for each 2km stretch I would think about a woman who
inspires me, dedicating that part of the ride to her. Because
she had given me the idea, I started with Hannah. I thought
about all the many ways in which she has enriched my
thinking, as an athlete and as a writer and as an intelligent
and inquisitive human being. I tried to remember everything
she'd told me about her Ironman preparation, optimistic that
I might be able to wring out a few more drops of wisdom to
help me with the task at hand. I filled my head with pride for
what she had accomplished the previous day, and wondered
how she was feeling in the aftermath, and looked forward
to the day, sometime in the hazy future, when all of this
would be over, and we'd meet up again, perhaps with wine
instead of tap water, and compare notes on what we'd been
through. I remembered that she, possibly more than anyone
else, is one of the people who, in the last year or so, have
helped me to realise that 'sports writing' need not be the dull,
brainless thing it is often reputed to be – that in fact it has
the potential to be the most interesting subject in the world,
dealing as it does with that intriguing interplay between the
human body and the human mind, a relationship still grossly
under-examined. I replayed a comment she'd made once,
in response to someone else's remark about 'keeping on

through the pain' of endurance sports. It's not about physical pain, she said, not unless you're pushing through an injury – it's more of a *striving tension*. She was right: I knew it then and I knew it even more now, at this moment, on the slopes of Ventoux. It's not a matter of enduring pain. It's much more subtle than that. No part of me was actually hurting at this moment, despite the ever-present urge to stop. And why, indeed, did I *want* to stop when the only way I could conceive of getting myself out of this was to keep going? "I can't go on, I'll go on." (Bit of Samuel Beckett for you.) *Striving tension*. I couldn't have put it better. Still can't.

I must have missed a kilometre marker, because the next one I passed told me I was 3km in. Only 18 to go from here. It was now a work in progress.

I thought about Hannah for one more kilometre, thanking her for helping me find a way up the mountain, wondering how she must have felt in the eleventh hour of her Ironman, still with most of a marathon ahead of her, wondering whether her own thought strategy had played out. I visualised her sending me some of the strength she was no longer using, since today, in the aftermath, all she was likely to be doing was sitting, lying, eating and drinking.

At the next kilometre marker I stopped, stretched, peed, caught my breath. I was in no hurry. The sun had now sunk completely behind the low horizon to the west, and the colour was draining from the sky. A couple of cyclists sped down the mountain, doubtless on their way back to their home or hotel, for a shower, clean clothes, dinner, a glass of wine, bed. I wondered what they thought of me, heading foolishly up towards the summit as night fell. They disappeared off towards Bédoin, and the road was quiet once again.

Note from Hannah: Read on here: thatemilychappell.com/2015/09/transcontinental-night-on-bald-mountain/ or search the title and her name. And buy her books! She's excellent.

The end.

Bibliography

Adams, M. (2011, Aug 25). *Edgelands – Matt Adams provocation.* (H. Nicklin, Editor) Retrieved Apr 8, 2012 from YouTube: http://www.youtube.com/watch?v=SGBtjCHGmiU

Fynsk, C. (1991). Foreword "Experiences of Finitude". In J.-L. Nancy, & P. Connor (Ed.), *The Inoperative Community* (P. Connor, L. Garbus, M. Holland, & a. S. Sawhney, Trans.). Minneapolis: University of Minnesota Press.

Joris, P. (1988). Translator's Preface. In M. Blanchot, & B. NY (Ed.), *The Unavowable Community* (P. Joris, Trans.). Station Hill Press Inc.

Kershaw, B. (1992). *The Politics of Performance: Radical theatre as cultural intervention.* London: Routledge.

Nancy, J.-L. (1991). *The Inoperative Community.* (P. Connor, Ed., P. Connor, L. Garbus, M. Holland, & S. Sawhney, Trans.) Minneapolis: University of Minnesota Press.

Turner, V. (1976). Social Dramas and Ritual Metaphors. In R. Schechner, & M. Schuman (Eds.), *Ritual, Play, and Performance: Readings in the Social Sciences/Theatre.* New York: The Seabury Press.

Watt, D. (2009). Performing, Strolling, Thinking: From Minor Literature to Theatre of the Future . In L. Cull (Ed.), *Deleuze and Performance* (pp. 91-101). Edinburgh: Edinburgh University Press.

Hannah Nicklin is a writer, game designer, academic and artist working at the confluence of devising, community-based practices and digital art and game design.

Hannah's work is often driven by an interest in the role of storytelling in everyday life; in enabling players, audiences and participants to reflect on their lives, lived in the inextricable context of one another. She works hard to make performance/ playful experiences that can be accessed by everybody, proactively, by taking work into communities, by producing and programming experimental work, and by being a bridge between creative. She also lectures in socially engaged practices, digital narrative and game design at several universities.